NEW TESTAMENT GREEK PRIMER

COMPANION TEXTS FOR NEW TESTAMENT STUDIES

A Critical Lexicon and Concordance to the English-Greek New Testament (Bullinger)

A Dictionary of New Testament Greek Synonyms (Berry)

A Grammar of Septuagint Greek (Conybeare and Stock)

A Greek-English Lexicon of the New Testament and Other Early Christian Literature (Bauer, Arndt, Gingrich, and Danker)

A Greek Grammar of the New Testament and Other Early Christian Literature (Blass and Debrunner, Funk)

A Linguistic Key to the Greek New Testament (Rienecker, Rogers)

A Reader's Greek-English Lexicon of the New Testament (Kubo)

A Shorter Lexicon of the Greek New Testament (Gingrich)

An Index to Bauer, Arndt, Gingrich, Greek Lexicon — 2nd Edition (Alsop)

Do It Yourself Hebrew and Greek (Goodrick)

Greek-English Lexicon to the New Testament (Greenfield, Green)

Greek-English Lexicon of the New Testament (Thayer)

New Testament Greek Primer (Marshall)

The Analytical Greek Lexicon Revised (Moulton)

The Englishman's Greek Concordance of the New Testament (Wigram)

The Englishman's Greek New Testament (Newberry)

The Greek New Testament Slidaverb Conjugation Chart (Peterson)

The Interlinear Greek-English New Testament (Berry)

The Interlinear Greek-English New Testament (Marshall)

The New International Dictionary of New Testament Theology (Brown)

The NIV Interlinear Greek-English New Testament (Marshall)

The RSV Interlinear Greek-English New Testament (Marshall)

The Zondervan Parallel New Testament in Greek and English (Marshall)

NEW TESTAMENT GREEK PRIMER

THE REV. ALFRED MARSHALL
D.Litt.

Academie
Books Grand Rapids, Michigan
Zondervan Publishing House

NEW TESTAMENT GREEK PRIMER
Copyright © 1962 by Alfred Marshall

ACADEMIE BOOKS are printed by Zondervan
Publishing House, 1415 Lake Drive, S.E.,
Grand Rapids, Michigan 49506

Reprinted by special arrangement with
Samuel Bagster & Sons Ltd.

ISBN 0-310-20401-1

All rights reserved. No portion of this book
may be reproduced in any form
without written permission of the publishers.

Printed in the United States of America

84 85 86 87 88 89 90 / 17 16 15 14 13 12 11

INTRODUCTION

This Primer of New Testament Greek, by one who has had some years of tutorial experience, and is responsible for the interlinear translation in the publishers' *Interlinear Greek-English New Testament*, is offered as a compact introduction for those who wish to acquire a working knowledge of the language. Such, on working through it, should be able to recognize any form of a Greek verb as found in the New Testament. The other parts of speech are also dealt with, and elementary syntactical principles are introduced by means of some twenty rules interspersed as the accidence proceeds, with adequate examples from the New Testament.

T. S. Green's *A Greek-English Lexicon to the New Testament* is available from the same publishers, giving sufficient guidance as to meanings, also with references to passages.

The numbering of paragraphs in this Primer makes it easy to refer backward and/or forward for other teaching on any given matter.

'A little and often' is a good practice for acquiring familiarity with these 'words taught of the spirit'.

A. MARSHALL

NEW TESTAMENT GREEK
PRIMER

PRELIMINARY

1. A literary work is built up of (1) LETTERS; these are formed into (2) WORDS; these, again, are arranged in (3) SEN-TENCES. So that a study of Greek must take this threefold form. Letters, once learnt, form the basis of all else and can be disposed of as mastered once for all. Unless, however, study is to be for a long while an uninteresting grind, we must become familiar with the construction of simple sentences at least as soon as the necessary words are known.

To put the matter in another way: we have to learn (1) ORTHOGRAPHY, (2) ACCIDENCE, and (3) SYNTAX. The first must be learnt outright, before anything else can be understood; but the other two can be studied side by side.

THE GREEK ALPHABET

2. The Greek alphabet consists of 24 letters—7 vowels and 17 consonants.

CAPITAL	SMALL	NAME	VALUE
A	α	*alpha*	a
B	β	*beta*	b
Γ	γ	*gamma*	g
Δ	δ	*delta*	d
E	ε	*epsilon*	e (short)
Z	ζ	*zeta*	z (= dz)
H	η	*eta*	e (long)
Θ	θ	*theta*	th
I	ι	*iota*	i
K	κ	*kappa*	k
Λ	λ	*lambda*	l
M	μ	*mu*	m
N	ν	*nu*	n
Ξ	ξ	*xi*	x
O	ο	*omicron*	o (short)
Π	π	*pi*	p
P	ρ	*rho*	r
Σ	σ or ς	*sigma*	s
T	τ	*tau*	t
Y	υ	*upsilon*	u
Φ	φ	*phi*	ph
X	χ	*chi*	ch
Ψ	ψ	*psi*	ps
Ω	ω	*omega*	o (long)

VOWELS

3. The vowels may be set out thus:

The centre three may be either long or short; the two on the left are always short; and to these correspond the two on the right, always long. The distinction between long and short vowels will be seen later on to be important.

Note the following syllables, pronouncing them as the English words given:

με*ν*—m*en*	τη*ν*—t*een*
ὀ*ν*—*on*	τω*ν*—t*one*

DIPHTHONGS

4.
αι—ai in *ai*sle
αυ—au in n*augh*t
ει—ei in h*eig*ht
οι—oi in *oi*l
ου—ou in thr*ou*gh
ευ, ηυ—eu in n*eu*ter
υι—we in bet*we*en

In addition, ι is written under (*iota subscriptum*) a long vowel (but by the side of a capital), as ᾳ, ῃ, ῳ (*Aι, Hι, Ωι*); it is then silent, only the long vowel being sounded:

τῳ—*tow*   τῃ—*tee*

BREATHINGS

5. If a Greek word begins with a vowel, that vowel has a 'breathing' over it; if with a diphthong, the second vowel has the breathing. There are two breathings—the smooth, or *spiritus lenis* ('); and the rough, or *spiritus asper* ('). The former makes no difference to the pronunciation, but the latter is represented by our *h*. Hence pronounce—

εἰς—*ice*   ἑν—*hen*

6. Initial *upsilon* always has the rough breathing, as ὑπό. Moreover, initial *rho* also always has it, as ῥῆμα; and double *rho* in the body of a word is written ῤῥ—that is, the first has the smooth and the second the rough breathing.

7. Occasionally, a breathing will be met with in the middle of a word; this shows that two words have been contracted into one, the first ending in a vowel and the second beginning with one.

Examples: κἀγώ = καὶ ἐγώ (and I); ταὐτά = τὰ αὐτά (the same things). This is called 'crasis'.

CONSONANTS

8. These present no difficulty in pronunciation, except that γ before another guttural (see para. 9) has the nasal sound of *ng*; thus, ἄγκυρα—*angkura*. Note the two forms of *sigma*: σ initial or medial, but ς when final. In such a case as εἰςφέρω, found in some editions of N.T., etc., the final ς is retained because εἰς is itself a word; this is simply a matter of editorial judgement. σ before β or μ is flat, not sharp (cp. our 'dismal'); hence pronounce κόσμος 'kozmoss'; ἄσβεστος 'azbesstoss.'

9. The classification of consonants according to their nature is important. Thus, of the 17—

4 (λ, μ, ν, ρ) are *liquids*;

3 (γ, κ, χ) are *gutturals*—formed in the throat;

3 (β, π, φ) are *labials*—formed with the lips;

3 (δ, τ, θ) are *dentals*—formed with the teeth;

1 (s or σ) is the *sibilant*; and

3 (ξ, ψ, ζ) are *double letters*, being the combination of a guttural, a labial, and a dental respectively with the sibilant: γs, κs, or χs = ξ; βs, πs, or φs = ψ; δs, τs, or θs = ζ.

10. The gutturals, labials, and dentals together constitute the 9 mutes, and these are cross-divided as shown in the columns of the following table, from which their mutual interrelationship may be seen:

	FLAT	SHARP	ASPIRATE
Gutturals	γ	κ	χ
Labials	β	π	φ
Dentals	δ	τ	θ

The important point to bear in mind in this connection is that when two of these mutes come together—*e.g.* a labial and a dental—they must be of the same order: both flat, or both sharp, or both aspirate, the former of the two being changed so as to bring it into harmony, so to speak, with the other—they must not be 'unequally yoked together'! The only exception is in words compounded with ἐκ. Hence γθ is an impossible combination—it must be χθ, both aspirates; we cannot have πδ—it would have to be βδ, both flats.

ACCENTS

11. The student at this stage need not concern him or her self greatly with the accents. There are three: the *acute* ('), the *grave* (`), and the *circumflex* (῀), which is a combination of an acute and a grave, in that order, but not of a grave and an acute. The circumflex can stand only over a long vowel, therefore never over ϵ or o; but the acute and the grave may stand on any vowel. In theory, every syllable of a Greek word is accented, but the grave accent is not printed unless it represents an acute. With certain exceptions, every word has one acute accent, which must be on one of the last three syllables, if the last syllable is short, but on either of the last two if the last is long. If the last syllable itself has the acute, then, if an accented word follows, the grave accent is used; thus καί (and), but καὶ ἐγένετο (and it happened). The actual place of the accent must be generally noted from each word as learnt; but verbs, with certain exceptions, throw the accent back as far as possible (note, *e.g.*, the two verbs in para. 14 below). Sometimes the different accentuation of words spelt alike shows a difference of meaning, as ἡ (the), but ἥ (who). In a diphthong the accent stands on the second vowel.

This is all that need be known now; particular points will be noted in due course.

DIACRITICAL MARKS

12. Apart from the accents, there are three diacritical marks to be noted.

(*a*) The *apostrophe* ('). This, as in English, etc., shows the omission of a letter. If a word—generally a preposition—ends in a vowel, and the word following begins with a vowel, the former may drop its vowel (but περί and some other words never do).

Example: δι᾽ ὧν = διὰ ὧν. If, however, this leaves a sharp mute before a rough breathing, the sharp is changed into its corresponding aspirate.

Example: ἀνθ᾽ ὧν = ἀντ᾽ ὧν = ἀντὶ ὧν. This is called ‘elision’, and is to be distinguished from crasis (para. 7).

(b) The *diæresis* (¨). This, appearing over the second of two vowels, indicates that both are to be pronounced—that is, that the two vowels do not form a diphthong.

Examples: Ἠσαΐας, πρωΐ.

(c) The mark, like a smooth breathing ('), which is the sign of crasis having taken place (para. 7), is called a *coronis*.

PUNCTUATION

13. There are four marks of punctuation in use.

(a) The *comma* (,), the use of which is pretty much the same as in English.

(b) The *full-stop* (.), also used as by ourselves.

(c) The *interrogation mark* (;)—that is, our semi-colon.

(d) The *colon* or *semi-colon* (·)—a full-stop in line with the top of the letters.

This disposes of the first division of our studies—letters, or orthography (see para. 1); we may now turn our attention to words, and then to sentences.

INFLEXION

14. Greek is an inflected or synthetic language, and is, in fact, the most perfect specimen of that class of language. English, on the other hand, as compared with Anglo-Saxon, has now become almost entirely analytic, having lost nearly all the inflexions it once possessed. The difference between the two classes of language is this: an analytic language builds up a phrase by the juxtaposition of separate words; whereas a synthetic language, starting with a stem containing a basic idea, modifies that stem until the desired thought is expressed.

Examples:

$$\text{Noun} \begin{cases} \text{man} = \dot{\alpha}\nu\acute{\eta}\rho = \text{Lat. } vir \\ \text{of man} = \dot{\alpha}\nu\delta\rho\acute{o}s = \quad viri \end{cases}$$

$$\text{Verb} \begin{cases} \text{I love} = \phi\iota\lambda\acute{\epsilon}\omega = amo \\ \text{I shall be loved} = \phi\iota\lambda\eta\theta\acute{\eta}\sigma o\mu\alpha\iota = amabor \end{cases}$$

The position may be illustrated by the few survivals of inflection in English. Thus, we modify the present 'I love' in order to express the indefinite past 'I loved', in the case of a weak verb, or we alter the radical vowel in 'I run' to express the same tense ('I ran') in the case of a strong verb. From 'who' as the nominative subject, we form 'whom' for the accusative or other case—that is, after a verb or a preposition.

15. Now what is thus done occasionally in English is done generally in Greek; and this process of inflexion is of two kinds:

(i) Verbs are *conjugated* to express—

    (*a*) Voice,

    (*b*) Mood,

    (*c*) Tense,

    (*d*) Number, and

    (*e*) Person.

(ii) Nouns, participles, adjectives, pronouns, the definite article, and some numerals are *declined* to express—

    (*a*) Number,

    (*b*) Case, and/or

    (*c*) Gender.

Note that the participle, being a part of the verb, falls into both processes.

All other parts of speech are uninflected—that is to say, they never change their form; they are therefore not included in this Primer, but must be learnt from a lexicon.

There are two conjugations of verbs, and three declensions of nouns, etc. We shall deal with the declensions first.

DECLENSION

16. By the *case* of a noun is shown its relation to other words in the sentence; by its *number* is indicated whether there is only one thing or person in question, or more than one; and a noun has its grammatical *gender*, which must not be confused with ideas of sex. There are five cases—nominative, accusative, vocative, genitive, and dative; in classical Greek there were three numbers—singular, dual, and plural, but the dual is not used in N.T.; and there are three genders—masculine, feminine, and neuter. If we take what is known as the definite article (though it has other functions) we shall see the various forms which it assumes, though here there is no vocative case.

THE DEFINITE ARTICLE

17.

		Singular			*Plural*	
	M.	F.	N.	M.	F.	N.
N.	ὁ	ἡ	τό	οἱ	αἱ	τά
A.	τόν	τήν	τό	τούς	τάς	τά
G.	τοῦ	τῆς	τοῦ	τῶν	τῶν	τῶν
D.	τῷ	τῇ	τῷ	τοῖς	ταῖς	τοῖς

This paradigm should be thoroughly memorized, and four points in it specially noted:

(i) The gen. pl. ends in -ων for all genders, and this will be seen to be true also of all declensions of nouns, etc., without exception.

(ii) The dat. sing. ends in -ι for all genders, and this too is true of all declensions, with the solitary exception of the proper name Ἰησοῦς. Here, and in the 1st and 2nd decl., this ι is subscript, because of the long vowel preceding; whereas in the 3rd decl. it is otherwise.

(iii) In the neuter, the nom. and acc. cases are alike in each number, and in the plural the ending is -α. This is so with all neuters, the vocative also agreeing. (In Latin also, neuter plurals end in -a.)

(iv) All the above forms consist of one syllable only, and this is characteristic of the 1st and 2nd decl., which are called 'parisyllabic', because all the cases of each noun have the same number of syllables; in the 3rd decl. the cases other than the nom. sing. have one syllable more than it, and this declension is therefore said to be 'imparisyllabic'.

The declension of the definite article, thoroughly mastered, will be found to give a general idea of the first two declensions of nouns.

FIRST DECLENSION OF NOUNS

18. The 1st decl. is known as the A declension, because the stem—that part of the word which can be recognized through all its forms, and to which the various endings are attached, with or without alteration—ends in α. It will be seen to resemble the fem. def. art. (para. 17) in the final syllable. There are the following five models:

Feminine nouns—

(a) the nominative ending in η (*i.e.* the α of the stem lengthened), this η being kept throughout the singular.

(b) the nom. reproducing the α of the stem, but changing to η in gen. and dat. when preceded by any consonant except ρ.

(c) the α of the stem retained throughout when it follows a vowel or ρ.

Masculine nouns—

(d) s added to η, which appears instead of α after any consonant except ρ.

(e) s added to the stem for the nom.

There are no neuter nouns in the 1st decl.

(*a*) γραφή = writing; stem—γραφα.

	Singular	Plural
N.	γραφή	γραφαί
A.	γραφήν	γραφάς
G.	γραφῆς	γραφῶν
D.	γραφῇ	γραφαῖς

(*b*) βασίλισσα = queen; stem—βασιλισσα.

N.	βασίλισσα	βασίλισσαι
A.	βασίλισσαν	βασιλίσσας
G.	βασιλίσσης	βασιλισσῶν
D.	βασιλίσσῃ	βασιλίσσαις

(*c*) θύρα = door; stem—θυρα.

N.	θύρα	θύραι
A.	θύραν	θύρας
G.	θύρας	θυρῶν
D.	θύρᾳ	θύραις

(*d*) κλέπτης = thief; stem—κλεπτα.

N.	κλέπτης	κλέπται
A.	κλέπτην	κλέπτας
G.	κλέπτου	κλεπτῶν
D.	κλέπτῃ	κλέπταις

(e) νεανίας = young man; stem—νεανια.

N.	νεανίας	νεανίαι
A.	νεανίαν	νεανίας
G.	νεανίου	νεανιῶν
D.	νεανίᾳ	νεανίαις

This is the only noun of this model.

The plural endings, it will be noticed, are the same for all five models, and the gen. pl. always ends in ῶν. In the masculine nouns (d) and (e) the masc. gen. sing. ending ου, as seen in the def. art. and the 2nd decl., appears. Note the instances in which the accent has to come forward owing to the last syllable being long (para. 11).

SECOND DECLENSION

19. The 2nd decl. is known as the O declension, because the stem ends in o. It will be seen to resemble the masc. and neut. def. art. respectively (para. 17). Two models only exist.

Masculine and feminine nouns—
   (a) adding s to the stem.

Neuter nouns—
   (b) adding ν to the stem.

(a) λόγος = word; stem—λογο.

	Singular	*Plural*
N.	λόγος	λόγοι
A.	λόγον	λόγους
G.	λόγου	λόγων
D.	λόγῳ	λόγοις

(b) ἔργον = work; stem—ἐργο.

N. A.	ἔργον	ἔργα
G.	ἔργου	ἔργων
D.	ἔργῳ	ἔργοις

20. There are only a score or so nouns which, though ending in oς and belonging to this declension, are feminine in gender (para. 32). Nothing else has to be learnt in connection with them, as they are declined exactly like λόγος.

21. These paradigms should be carefully studied in the light of the general principles laid down in para. 17, to see how those principles work out. Much perplexity will thereby be obviated. For purposes of accentuation, the diphthongs αι and οι in the nom. pl. in these two declensions are reckoned to be short.

THE USE OF THE CASES

22. (i) The *nominative* is the case of the subject—the doer of an action, or that of which something is asserted or predicated (para. 43).

Example:

The slave   not remains (John 8. 35)

ὁ   δοῦλος   οὐ   μένει

'The slave' is here that of which it is affirmed that he 'remains not', and hence is in the nominative.

(ii) The *accusative* is the case of the direct object—that which suffers the action described by the active verb.

Example:

I love   *God* (1 John 4. 20)

ἀγαπῶ   τὸν   Θεόν

'God' is here the direct object of the verb 'love', and hence is in the accusative case. This case is governed by certain prepositions.

(iii) The *genitive* is usually expressed in English by the

preposition 'of' or 'from'; but the student should be on his guard against the mistaken notion that it must always be so rendered—this is simply a convenient way of indicating the ideas of ablation, partition, and relation conveyed by the case. In Greek it is always used after certain prepositions, which are said to 'govern' that case; and certain verbs also require the genitive case to be used with them.

Example:

The word *of God* (Rev. 19. 13)

ὁ   λόγος   τοῦ   Θεοῦ

'Of', implying possession, is not expressed by a separate word, but the genitive case indicates, *inter alia*, possession. 'God', in N.T., commonly, but not invariably, has the def. art. There is also the construction called the 'genitive absolute', which will be dealt with in due course (para. 153).

(iv) The *dative* is usually expressed in English by 'to', but the same remark applies here as to the gen. 'On' or 'at' must sometimes be used, as in ideas of time; also 'in' or 'with'. It is also governed by prepositions, and again by certain verbs. ('The dative is diametrically opposed to the genitive.'   Farrar, *Brief Greek Syntax*, p. 71.)

Example:

He said   *to the paralytic* (Luke 5. 24)

εἶπεν   τῷ   παραλελυμένῳ

(v) In addition, the *vocative* is the case used in addressing a person, though the student must be prepared to find the nom. so used, with or without ὦ.

Example:

O   *man!* (Rom. 2. 1)

ὦ   ἄνθρωπε

As, however, it is seldom used, and anyhow is always the same in the pl. as the nom., it is not considered worth while to take up space in giving it separately: κύριε (O Lord), Θεέ (O God), ἄνθρωπε (O man), γυναί (O woman), are almost the only forms found in the N.T.

Notice that the nominative is not governed by prepositions or verbs—it is itself the governing word in a sentence; for the key to every sentence is in its nominative subject. Neither, of course, is the vocative. All cases other than the nominative are called 'oblique' cases. Precisely the same remarks apply, obviously, to the plural number as to the singular.

23. Rule 1. *The article must agree with the noun to which it belongs in gender, number, and case.*

VOCABULARIES

These are given for practice and obviously are only selective. A lexicon must be consulted for further words.

24. *Feminine Nouns of the 1st Decl.:* ἀγάπη, love; ἁμαρτία, sin; ἀρχή, beginning; βασιλεία, kingdom; γῆ, earth, land; γλῶσσα, tongue; δικαιοσύνη, righteousness; δόξα, glory; εἰρήνη, peace; ἐντολή, commandment; ἐξουσία, right, authority; ζωή, life; καρδία, heart; κεφαλή, head; νεφέλη, cloud; οἰκία, house (strictly the whole house—see οἶκος, para. 26); ὀργή, wrath; σοφία, wisdom; χώρα, country; ψυχή, soul, life.

25. *Masculine Nouns of the 1st Decl.:* δεσπότης, master; κριτής, judge; λῃστής, robber; μαθητής, disciple; προφήτης, prophet; στρατιώτης, soldier.

26. *Masculine Nouns of the 2nd Decl.:* ἄγγελος, messenger, angel; ἄνθρωπος, man (human being = Lat. *homo* = Ger. *Mensch*); βωμός, (heathen) altar; ἀπόστολος, apostle; γάμος, wedding, marriage; διδάσκαλος, teacher; ἥλιος, sun; θρόνος, throne; ναός, temple (the holy places, the inner shrines—see ἱερόν, para. 27); νόμος, law; οἶκος, house (strictly, set of rooms—see οἰκία, para. 24); οὐρανός, heaven (always plural in Mat.); σταυρός, cross; υἱός, son; Χρίστος, Christ.

27. *Neuter Nouns of the 2nd Decl.:* δένδρον, tree; δῶρον, gift; εὐαγγέλιον, gospel; ἱερόν, temple (the whole building—see ναός, para. 26); τέκνον, child.

28. ἐν, in, among, by; σύν, with; ἀλλά, but; καί, and, also, even; οὐ (οὐκ before an unaspirated, οὐχ before an aspirated, vowel), not (this is the categorical negative, used when matters of fact are in question).

EXERCISE 1

Turn into Greek:

The gifts of the prophet. The queen's soldiers (*i.e.* the soldiers of the queen). Life and peace (abstract nouns may take the def. art.). The doors of the temple. The prophet's children. The master of the house. God's commandments. O queen. The cross of Christ. The sins of the tongue. The trees of the earth. The words of the teachers. Speak (λέξον) to the men.

Into the framework of the paradigms given (paras. 18, 19) of the 1st and 2nd decl. a number of special forms must be fitted.

FIRST DECLENSION
Special Forms

29. Proper names ending in ας form the gen. in α instead of ου if a consonant precedes the stem letter; otherwise they follow νεανίας. Κηφᾶς = Cephas, gen. Κηφᾶ. Ἀνδρέας = Andrew, gen. Ἀνδρέου. To the former class belong also—

βορρᾶς = north, μαμωνᾶς = mammon. Μνᾶ = pound follows θύρα. A few nouns in ρα have gen. and dat. like βασίλισσα, but editions of N.T. vary somewhat in these words.

SECOND DECLENSION

Special Forms

30. The proper name Ἰησοῦς = Jesus (para. 17 (ii)) belongs here, its spelling being due to its Hebrew derivation: A. Ἰησοῦν; G., D. Ἰησοῦ. Ἀπολλώς = Apollos has—A. Ἀπολλών or Ἀπολλώ; G. Ἀπολλώ.

INDECLINABLE NOUNS

31. There are a number of proper names in the Greek Scriptures taken over from their Hebrew originals. In some instances these are more or less adapted to the genius of the Greek language, and are declined (paras. 29, 30); but in others this is not so, and they are left undeclined, only the article indicating the case. Such are Ἰσραήλ, Δαβίδ, etc. One proper name in particular should be noted here, occurring as it does in three different forms: (i) Ἰερουσαλήμ, indeclinable; (ii) Ἱεροσόλυμα, neut. pl., 2nd decl.; (iii) Ἱεροσόλυμα, fem. sing., 1st decl.—? Mat. 2. 3 only.

VOCABULARY

32. *Feminine Nouns in* ος *of the 2nd Decl.* (complete list—see para. 20): ἄβυσσος, abyss; ἄμμος, sand; ἄμπελος, vine; βίβλος, book, roll; διάλεκτος, language; δοκός, beam (of wood); εἴσοδος, entrance; ἔξοδος, exit; ἔρημος, wilderness; κάμηλος,* camel; κιβωτός, ark; ληνός,* winepress; λιμός,* famine; μόσχος,* calf; νῆσος, island; ὁδός, way; ὄνος,* ass;

* = sometimes masculine.

παρθένος, virgin; περίχωρος, region round about; ῥάβδος, staff, sceptre, rod; τρίβος, path.

33. No noun of the 1st or 2nd decl. should now present any difficulty. One anticipatory warning, however, may save students some perplexity: there are a number of nouns whose nominative ends in ος, but which belong to the 3rd decl. and are neuter in gender (para. 83); these must be distinguished from nouns in ος belonging to the 2nd decl. (para. 19 (a)); the gender will indicate their classification.

34. Rule 2. *The prepositions ἐν (in, by) and σύν (with) always govern the dative case.*

35. Rule 3. *All words between an article and the noun to which it belongs must be taken therewith as together forming one phrase.* Thus, for the first of the expressions set for translation in Exercise 1, τὰ τοῦ προφήτου δῶρα is perfectly good Greek, the neut. pl. def. art. τά being taken with the neut. pl. noun δῶρα = the gifts; then the dependent genitives in between = of the prophet. An instance of this idiom occurs in Luke 3. 2, τὸν Ζαχαρίου υἱόν = the son (acc.) of Zacharias. This usage sometimes determines the interpretation of a passage.

EXERCISE 2

English words in italic in the exercises are to be expressed in Greek. Words in square brackets are not required in the Greek.

Turn into Greek:

In the clouds of *the* heaven. The kingdom of heaven (say, of the heavens). In the way of God's commandments. The gospel of Jesus Christ. The disciple said to *the* Jesus (see para. 22 (iv)). In the law and the prophets. The prophet's staff. The paths of righteousness. The peace of God. In the region round about.

PERSONAL PRONOUNS

36. *First Person:*

	Singular	Plural
N.	ἐγώ, I	ἡμεῖς, we
A.	ἐμέ or με, me	ἡμᾶς, us
G.	ἐμοῦ or μου, of me	ἡμῶν, of us
D.	ἐμοί or μοι, to me	ἡμῖν, to us

37. *Second Person:*

N.	σύ, thou	ὑμεῖς, ye
A.	σέ or σε, thee	ὑμᾶς, you
G.	σοῦ or σου, of thee	ὑμῶν, of you
D.	σοί or σοι, to thee	ὑμῖν, to you

As a mnemonic aid for the pl. forms, it may be noted that the initial vowel of the Greek rhymes with the respective English equivalent—ἡμεῖς, we; ὑμεῖς, you. The gen. pl. still ends in ων, and the dat. sing. in ι; see para. 17 (i) and (ii). An idiomatic use of the gen. should be carefully noticed:

τὰ πρόβατά μου = the sheep of-me = my sheep

38. *Third Person.* Strictly speaking, there is no 3rd pers. pron. in Greek. An adjective-pronoun, meaning 'self', does duty, and when so used has the meaning assigned: αὐτός (he), αὐτή (she), αὐτό (it). As it is declined exactly like, *e.g.*, λόγος, γραφή, and τό, respectively, no paradigm need be set out. The accent should be particularly noted.

Here, too, the gen. is used idiomatically:

τὸ τέκνον αὐτῆς = the child of-her = her child
αἱ ἁμαρτίαι αὐτῶν = the sins of-them = their sins

As in English, there is no distinction of gender in the 1st and 2nd pers., but there is in the 3rd.

THE VERB 'TO BE'

39. Not much can be done without calling on the verb 'to be', so that at this point forms of εἶναι (to be) should be learnt. This verb connotes the simple fact of being, and is to be distinguished from another verb which means 'to become'. The form of the verb includes the notion of the pers. pron. (cp. Span. *tengo*, I have), which, therefore, is expressed only when emphasis is intended.

Present Indicative:

Singular	Plural
εἰμί, I am	ἐσμέν, we are
εἶ, thou art	ἐστέ, ye are
ἐστί(ν), he, she, *or* it is	εἰσί(ν), they are

In the 3rd pers., sing. and pl., the ν (*nu* suffixed) may or may not be found; editions of N.T. vary.

40. *Imperfect Indicative:*

Singular	Plural
ἦν, I was	ἦμεν, we were
ἦς (*or* ἦσθα), thou wast	ἦτε, ye were
ἦν, he, she, *or* it was	ἦσαν, they were

41. *Future Indicative:*

Singular	Plural
ἔσομαι, I shall be	ἐσόμεθα, we shall be
ἔσῃ, thou shalt be	ἔσεσθε, ye shall be
ἔσται, he will be	ἔσονται, they will be

The 3rd pers. may be used in the impersonal sense: there is, etc.

42. Rule 4. *A verb must agree with its nominative case in number and person.* Nouns are in the 3rd pers., because, obviously, they are 'spoken of'. An exception to this in Greek is that a neuter plural may take a singular verb.

Examples:

Mat. 16. 18, σὺ εἶ Πέτρος = thou art Peter

In John 10 the neut. pl. τὰ πρόβατα occurs repeatedly with sing. verbs, though also with pl.; the matter is somewhat uncertain.

SENTENCES—I. SIMPLE

43. A sentence is a statement, if affirmative (either negatively or positively so), or a question, if interrogative, made about someone or something; or a thought expressed in words. For this a verb is usually necessary, though Greek idiom permits the copulative verb to be dispensed with in the construction 1 (*b*) below (see para. 54).

The essentials of a simple sentence are two—a *subject* (necessarily in the nominative case) and a *predicate*. The former is that about which something is affirmed, and the latter is that which is affirmed. The subject may be either (1) a noun or (2) a pronoun. The predicate may be (*a*) another noun, (*b*) an adjective, or (*c*) a verb. Note that the participle is a verbal adjective and the infinitive a verbal noun. Hence arise six possible constructions.

Examples:

1 (*a*) ὁ ἀγρός ἐστιν ὁ κόσμος (Mat. 13. 38)
    = the field is the world

1 (*b*) εὐλογητὸς ὁ Θεὸς καὶ πατὴρ κ.τ.λ. (Eph. 1. 3)
    = blessed is the God and Father, etc.

1 (*c*) Χριστὸς ὑπὲρ ἡμῶν ἀπέθανεν (Rom. 5. 8)
    = Christ died for us

2 (a) σὺ εἶ ὁ υἱὸς τοῦ Θεοῦ, σὺ βασιλεὺς εἶ τοῦ ᾿Ισραήλ
(John 1. 49)
= thou art the Son of God, thou art Israel's king

2 (b) οὗτος μέγας κληθήσεται ἐν τῇ βασιλείᾳ τῶν οὐρανῶν
(Mat. 5. 19)
= he shall be called great in the kingdom of heaven

2 (c) πρὶν ᾿Αβραὰμ γένεσθαι ἐγὼ εἰμί (John 8. 58)
= before Abraham came into being, I am

From such simple sentences all others are but a development.
It is necessary to distinguish between the verb 'to be' used
absolutely, or substantively, as in 2 (c) above, and copulatively,
as in 2 (a); also between transitive and intransitive verbs (or
the same verb used transitively and intransitively).

When two common nouns are in question, Greek distin-
guishes between subject and predicate by marking the former
with the def. art.　If, as in 1 (a) above, both have the art.,
the proposition is said to be a 'convertible' one—i.e. the two
terms can change places without alteration of meaning.

An inflected language allows of greater variety in the order
of the words of a sentence than a non-inflected one; the case
of a noun, e.g., unmistakably shows its function.　So in Greek
—within limits—the order of words is a matter of style and
emphasis; the verb may come first or last, which are the two
emphatic positions.

SENTENCES—II. COMPOUND

44. The essence of a simple sentence, then, is that it should
contain one finite verb and one subject.　The subject may,
indeed, be a compound one:

(The master and his disciple) are in the temple
ὁ κύριος καὶ ὁ μαθητὴς αὐτοῦ εἰσιν ἐν τῷ ἱερῷ

Here the words in parentheses together constitute the one
compound subject of the predicate verb.

45. But as soon as two finite verbs are introduced a compound sentence results:

The boy runs and falls down

τὸ παιδίον τρέχει καὶ καταπίπτει

This sentence really = (the boy runs) and (the boy, or he, falls down); hence we have two simple sentences reduced to one compound sentence. On the other hand, two or more sentences, each 'simple' in itself, with different subjects, may be linked by a connective particle.

Example:

τὸν Ἰακὼβ ἠγάπησα, τὸν δὲ Ἡσαῦ ἐμίσησα (Rom. 9. 13)
= Jacob I loved, but Esau I hated.

VOCABULARY

46. ἀλήθεια, truth; κύριος, lord, master; ἀδελφή, sister; ἀδελφός, brother; παιδίον, lad, child; διδαχή, teaching, doctrine; καρπός, fruit; κόσμος, universe, world; σημεῖον, sign; τελώνης, tax-gatherer. (The student should exercise his knowledge on the gender and declension of these nouns.)

ἀντί, instead of, against; ἀπό, from, away from; ἐκ (ἐξ before a vowel), out, out of, of, from; πρό, before.

47. Rule 5. *A copulative verb takes the same case after it as before it.*

48. Rule 6. *The prepositions ἀντί, ἀπό, ἐκ (ἐξ before a vowel), and πρό always govern the genitive case.*

EXERCISE 3

A. Translate:

τὰ πρόβατά μου ἐν τῇ ἐρημῷ ἐστι. ἐγὼ Κύριος (Jehovah = 'the LORD' in A.V.) ὁ Θεὸς ὑμῶν. ἐγώ εἰμι ἡ ὁδὸς καὶ ἡ ἀλήθεια καὶ ἡ ζωή. ἐν τῷ υἱῷ αὐτοῦ Ἰησοῦ Χριστῷ ἐστε.

Ἰησοῦς ὁ υἱὸς τοῦ Θεοῦ ἐστιν. ἐγώ εἰμι τὸ Α καὶ τὸ Ω. ἐκ τοῦ Θεοῦ ἐσμεν; οὐκ ἐστὶν ὁ κόσμος ἐκ τοῦ Θεοῦ.

B. Turn into Greek:

Their children are in the house. Your sons are not in the island. Thou art in the kingdom of God. We are Christians. The gospel of Jesus Christ is with authority. The children of God are in the way of righteousness. Young man, thy heart is not in peace.

ENLARGEMENTS AND EXTENSIONS

49. The subject of a sentence may be *enlarged* by an adjective, a participial phrase, a prepositional phrase, or a relative sentence; these enlarge our knowledge of the subject. On the other hand, the predicate may be *extended*—if a verb, by a prepositional phrase or an adverb; if a noun, etc., as above for the subject; and so on. In such a sentence as that in para. 44, 'in the temple' is a prepositional phrase extending the predicative verb 'are'. These various grammatical terms, and others, will be dealt with in due course; for the present we may turn our attention to—

ADJECTIVES

50. Adjectives modify nouns, and are classified thus:

    (i) Qualifying,

    (ii) Possessive,

    (iii) Numeral, and

    (iv) Demonstrative.

QUALIFYING ADJECTIVES
First Form

51. If the student has thoroughly mastered the 1st and 2nd decl. of nouns, the first form of qualifying adjectives will present no difficulty whatever. They have three terminations (but see para. 52 below), for masc., fem., and neut.; and these follow the declension of nouns in ος, α or η, and ον respectively. If the stem ends in any consonant other than ρ, the fem. ends in η; if in ρ or a vowel, in α. Thus we have ἀγαθός, ἀγαθή, ἀγαθόν (good); and as its declension is quite regular, there is no need to set out a paradigm. Thus also ἅγιος, ἁγία, ἅγιον (holy), to which the same remark applies.

52. A few adjectives of the first form have two terminations only, having no distinct fem. termination, the masc. doing duty for the fem. as well. Others, again, vary between two and three. Allowance must be made for a margin of uncertainty as between various editions of the Scriptures in cases such as these.

53. Rule 7. *Adjectives must agree with the nouns they modify in number, gender* (subject, *e.g.*, to para. 52 above), *and case* (cp. Rule 1, para. 23).

ATTRIBUTIVE AND PREDICATIVE POSITIONS

54. It now becomes necessary to distinguish very carefully between the two positions in which an adjective may modify a noun.

In the phrase 'The just judge', the adj. 'just' is said to modify 'judge' in the *attributive* position, or attributively; but if we say, 'The judge is just', 'just', while still modifying 'judge', does so in the *predicative* position, or predicatively. (Students of German will appreciate this distinction.) Now in Greek each of these positions may be expressed in two ways:

ὁ κριτὴς ὁ δίκαιος ὁ δίκαιος κριτής	both mean 'the just judge'
ὁ κριτὴς δίκαιος δίκαιος ὁ κριτής	„ „ 'the judge is just'

It will be seen that with the adjective in the predicative position the copulative verb may be suppressed, and is so here; but the order of the words demands that we construe it thus, and not otherwise.   On the other hand, the copula may be expressed.

As to ὁ δίκαιος κριτής, cp. Rule 3, para. 35.

If the def. art. is not used, the adj. may precede or follow the noun.

ADJECTIVES AND ARTICLE AS NOUNS

55. A common mode of expression is that of an adjective being used without a noun expressed; the latter is understood— men, women, or things according to the gender of the adj. This occurs occasionally in English, as when we speak of 'the deaf'—'persons' is understood; but is much commoner in Greek.   Hence—

> τὰ ἄγαθα = the good things (*also* goods, wealth, blessings)
> οἱ σοφοί = the wise men *or* persons, those who are wise

56. The def. art. may also be used alone; τά = the things; οἱ = the persons, those, they.

IRREGULAR ADJECTIVES

57. There are two commonly used adjs., slightly irregular in the sing. only, which may be taken here.

'Great':

	M.	F.	N.
N.	μέγας	μεγάλη	μέγα
A.	μέγαν	μεγάλην	μέγα
G.	μεγάλου	μεγάλης	μεγάλου
D.	μεγάλῳ	μεγάλῃ	μεγάλῳ

The plural is regular—μέγαλοι, μέγαλαι, μέγαλα.

'Much':	M.	F.	N.
N.	πολύς	πολλή	πολύ
A.	πολύν	πολλήν	πολύ
G.	πολλοῦ	πολλῆς	πολλοῦ
D.	πολλῷ	πολλῇ	πολλῷ

The plural is regular—πολλοί, πολλαί, πολλά; but here the meaning is, of course, 'many'.

VOCABULARIES

58. *Qualifying Adjectives of the First Form* (if a distinct termination for the fem. occurs sometimes, but not always, it is given in parentheses): πιστός, ή, όν, faithful, trustworthy; σοφός, ή, όν, wise; οὐράνιος, (α), ον, heavenly; αἰώνιος, (α), ον, age-lasting, eternal; καλός, ή, όν, fair, good, noble; φρόνιμος, ον, prudent; τυφλός, ή, όν, blind; πονηρός, ά, όν, evil, bad (opp. of ἄγαθος) (ὁ πονηρός = the Wicked One, Satan; τὸ πονηρόν, evil); κακός, ή, όν, evil, wicked.

59. *Nouns*: οἰκουμένη, inhabited earth (? = the Roman Empire); ζῶον, living creature, animal; θηρίον, wild beast; ἐκκλησία, called-out gathering, church; πλοῖον, ship; ποταμός, river; θάλασσα, sea; ἵππος, horse.

EXERCISE 4

A. Translate:

πιστὸς ὁ λόγος. ζωὴ αἰώνιος ἐν τῷ υἱῷ τοῦ Θεοῦ ἐστιν. ἡ ἐκκλησία τοῦ Θεοῦ ἡ ἐν Χριστῷ Ἰησοῦ τῷ κυρίῳ ἡμῶν (the construction of this phrase is identical with the first in para. 54 above; translate the second ἡ by 'which (is)'). μεγάλη ἡ ἀγάπη τοῦ Θεοῦ. ἀγαθά ἐστι τὰ τοῦ Θεοῦ. οὐκ ἔσμεν ἐκ τοῦ πονηροῦ.

B. Turn into Greek:

The great things of my law. God's throne is in heaven. God is good. The judges are just. To the faithful in Christ Jesus. The blind man is before the door of the temple. With the wild beasts.

THE DATIVE OF POSSESSION

60. There is, naturally, a verb 'to have' in Greek, to which we shall come in due course. But it may be noted here that there is a way of expressing possession by using the verb 'to be' with the dative of the possessor (cp. Fr. *c'est à moi* = that is mine).

Example:

οὐκ ἦν αὐτοῖς τέκνον (Luke 1. 7)

= not was to-them a child = they had no child

POSSESSIVE ADJECTIVES

61. Then, in addition to the use of the genitive of the personal pronouns (paras. 36, 37) to indicate possession, there are—but for the 1st and 2nd pers. only—possessive adjectives:

First pers. sing. (my)—ἐμός, ἐμή, ἐμόν
    „   „   *pl.* (our)—ἡμέτερος, ἡμετέρα, ἡμέτερον

Second pers. sing. (thy)—σός, σή, σόν
    „   „   *pl.* (your)—ὑμέτερος, ὑμετέρα, ὑμέτερον

These adjectives are governed by the same syntactical rules as other adjectives (paras. 53–55; cp. also para. 51). It must be borne in mind that they agree, as in French, with the thing possessed, not with the possessor.

Examples:

ἡ ἡμετέρα ἡ κοινωνία (1 John 1. 3) = our fellowship;
τὰ ἐμά (John 17. 10) = my things.

The use of these possessive adjectives is not so frequent in N.T. as the genitive of the personal pronouns. The only possessive for the 3rd pers. in N.T. is the gen. of αὐτός (para. 38).

DEMONSTRATIVE ADJECTIVES

62. Still keeping to the models of the 1st and 2nd decl., we may now turn to demonstrative adjectives. As their name implies, they 'point out' a person or thing, expressed or understood. For the present we may concern ourselves with these four, requiring special notice:

    (1) ὅδε, ἥδε, τόδε, this (here)
    (2) οὗτος, αὕτη, τοῦτο, this (near)
    (3) ἐκεῖνος, ἐκείνη, ἐκεῖνο, that (yonder)
    (4) ὁ αὐτός, ἡ αὐτή, τὸ αὐτό, the same

63. (1) ὅδε is merely the def. art. declined with δέ.

Example: Rev. 2. 1, τάδε = these things (acc.)

64. (2) This must be very carefully distinguished from αὐτός (para. 38), especially in fem. nom. sing. and pl.; also ταῦτα (= these things) from ταὐτά (= the same things—paras. 7, 66). Its full declension is as follows:

| | *Singular* | | | *Plural* | | |
	M.	F.	N.	M.	F.	N.
N.	οὗτος	αὕτη	τοῦτο	οὗτοι	αὗται	ταῦτα
A.	τοῦτον	ταύτην	τοῦτο	τούτους	ταύτας	ταῦτα
G.	τούτου	ταύτης	τούτου	τούτων	τούτων	τούτων
D.	τούτῳ	ταύτῃ	τούτῳ	τούτοις	ταύταις	τούτοις

When οὗτος is used with a noun, the def. art. also is used, and then the dem. adj. precedes the art. or follows the noun. There may be a slight nuance of distinction, but this is one of those finer points which the student must be prepared to work out for himself in the light of fuller knowledge. Anyhow, we have—

Mat. 15. 8, ὁ λαὸς οὗτος⎫
Mark 7. 6, οὗτος ὁ λαός ⎭ = this people

65. (3) This is declined quite regularly, like a qualifying adjective of the first form. The same remark applies, as to def. art., as under οὗτος; but there are occasional exceptions.

66. (4) (cp. para. 38). Αὐτός, ἡ, ό, when immediately preceded by the def. art., means 'the same' and is then strictly an adjective, conforming to the rules for such (paras. 53–55).

Examples:

ὁ αὐτὸς κύριος (I Cor. 12. 5) = the same lord
ἡ χώρα ἡ αὐτή (Luke 2. 8) = the same country

67. There are also—

ἄλλος, η, ο, another (numerically) (note the accentuation, especially the neut. pl., ἄλλα (other things), distinguished from the conjunction ἀλλά (but)); ἕτερος, α, ον, another (of a different kind).

VOCABULARY

68. δοῦλος, slave; ἀνά, up; εἰς, into, in (sometimes indistinguishable from ἐν = in, though ἐν never = into); μετά, c. gen., with (cp. σύν), c. acc., after.

69. Rule 8. *The prepositions ἀνά and εἰς always govern the accusative case.*

EXERCISE 5

A. Translate:

οἱ δοῦλοι τοῦ πονηροῦ οὐκ εἰσιν καλοί.   μεγάλη ἡ δικαιοσύνη

σου. οἱ ἐν τῇ βασιλείᾳ τῶν οὐρανῶν οὐκ εἰσι κακοί. ἡ
ἡμετέρα δικαιοσύνη οὐκ ἔστιν ἐκ τοῦ νόμου. μαθητὴς τοῦ
διδασκάλου τοῦ μεγάλου ἔστιν. ὁ κύριός μου εἶ σύ. βίβλος
ἐστί μοι. τάδε εἶπεν ὁ κύριος. ἐν ἐκείνῳ τῷ οἴκῳ μέγας
προφήτης ἦν. μετὰ ταῦτα.

B. Express in Greek, each in three different ways:

Thy righteousness.   Our sons.   Your ships.   My disciples.

C. Render into Greek:

We had great peace.   That man will be a great teacher.   I
was a slave.   We were not in that country.   Thou art our
lord.

Αὐτός IN APPOSITION

70. There is one other use of αὐτός to be considered. It is
used 'in apposition'—*i.e.* referring to the same person or
things—with nouns, as well as with 1st and 2nd pers. prons.,
with which of course it must agree in number, gender, and case;
it then means 'self', and has (*a*) in the nom. an emphatic or
intensive, and/or (*b*) in the oblique cases a reflexive, force.

Examples:

αὐτὸς ἐγώ   = I myself (Rom. 7. 25)
αὐτὸς Ἰησοῦς = Jesus himself (Luke 24. 15)
αὐτοὶ ὑμεῖς   = you yourselves (1 Thes. 4. 9)

71. In the oblique cases of the 1st and 2nd pers. prons. sing.
(paras. 36, 37) the pron. and αὐτός are combined into one
word—ἐμαυτοῦ, σεαυτόν, etc. These forms are quite regular,
but obviously can occur only in the masc. and fem., as the
'person speaking' or the 'person spoken to' must be either a
man or a woman. In the pl. the two words are written
separately.

σῶσον σεαυτόν = save thyself (Luke 23. 37)
ὑμῶν αὐτῶν　 = your own (I Cor. 7. 35)

72. (a) In the 3rd pers. the form is ἑ + αὐτόν = ἑαυτόν, etc., throughout all the oblique cases, both numbers, and all three genders, as the 'person spoken of' may be a grammatical neuter, as well as otherwise.

Example:

τὰ περὶ ἑαυτοῦ = the-things concerning himself (Luke 24. 27)

The reflexive force of the pronoun is seen here, in that 'himself' refers back to the subject of the sentence—he (*i.e.*, Jesus).

(b) Where there is no risk of ambiguity, this reflexive pron. may be used for the 1st and 2nd pers.

Example:

τὴν ἑαυτῶν σωτηρίαν
= your own salvation (acc.) (Phil. 2. 12)

(c) It is sometimes written in a contracted form—αὑτόν, etc. (note rough breathing); but this is one of the moot points of N.T. orthography.

There are thus three uses of αὐτός to be carefully distinguished—see respectively paras. 38, 66, and 70. We may take leave of it by citing John 2. 24:

αὐτὸς ᾽Ιησοῦς οὐκ ἐπίστευεν αὐτὸν αὐτοῖς
= Jesus himself did not entrust himself to them

Here αὐτός is in apposition with ᾽Ιησοῦς, the nom. subject of the sentence (para. 70); αὑτόν is the reflexive form (para. 72 (c)); and αὐτοῖς is the dat. pl. of the 3rd pers. use (para. 38).

THIRD DECLENSION

Introductory

73. In para. 17 (iv) it was laid down that a radical distinction
between the 1st and 2nd decl. and the 3rd is that the first two
are parisyllabic and the other imparisyllabic; and the student
will see that hitherto, whatever the number of syllables in the
nom. sing. of a noun or adjective, that number is found in all
the other cases. The same general rules still obtain (para.
17 (i)–(iii)), but it will now be found that the other cases may
have one syllable more. In addition, the dat. pl. always ends
in σι. It is of even greater importance now to know and
recognize the stem of a noun (see below, para. 74).

As the def. art. provided a model for the 1st and 2nd decl.,
so there is a type for the 3rd.

It may have been noticed that we have as yet had no
indefinite article—'a' or 'an'. There is, strictly speaking, no
such in Greek; but there is an indefinite adjective-pronoun
which does duty on occasion therefor, and this is the type for
the 3rd decl. of nouns. It means 'a certain', 'any', 'a', and
is declined thus:

INDEFINITE ADJECTIVE-PRONOUN

74.

	Singular		*Plural*	
	M. and F.	N.	M. and F.	N.
N.	τις	τι	τινες	τινα
A.	τινα	τι	τινας	τινα
G.	τινος	τινος	τινων	τινων
D.	τινι	τινι	τισι	τισι

The word is generally unaccented, as here, the accent being
thrown back on to the preceding word if the laws of Greek
accentuation allow. It may be accented in some positions—
acute, never grave, on the last syllable, or circumflex in gen. pl.

(τινῶν).   When accented on the stem syllable it is interrogative; τί = what? τίνος = of whom = whose?

Now the stem of this word is τιν, which is found by taking
away the syllable ος from the gen. sing.   *This is the governing
rule for the 3rd decl.* subject to a few easily understood modifications.   Further, before σ, ν is dropped; hence the nom. sing.
masc. and fem. and dat. pl. forms.   Neuters commonly drop
the final letter of the stem.   If this paradigm is mastered, no
insuperable difficulty will be encountered in the 3rd decl.,
which, as above stated, conforms to this type throughout.

The position of τις, when modifying a noun as an adjective,
is generally after, though it may precede, such: ἄνθρωπός
τις = a certain man (note accentuation).   But it cannot stand
as the first word of a sentence.

Paradigms

Nine models (**a–i**) may be distinguished, all conforming
to the type indicated in para. 74.

75. *Model* **a.**   Here we find the unaltered stem as the nom.,
and as the stem ends in a consonant the acc. is formed by
adding α.

αἰών (masc.) = age (cp. αἰώνιος); stem—αἰων

	Singular	*Plural*
N.	αἰών	αἰῶνες
A.	αἰῶνα	αἰῶνας
G.	αἰῶνος	αἰώνων
D.	αἰῶνι	αἰῶσι

76. *Model* **b.**   Very similar to **a** are those nouns in which
the vowel preceding the consonantal stem ending is lengthened
in the nom. sing.   It is not necessary to set out a paradigm,

as this is the only difference between the two models. Lexicons which give the gen. sing. thereby indicate the model.

Examples: ποιμήν (m.) = shepherd; stem—ποιμεν. ῥήτωρ (m.) = orator; stem—ῥητορ.

There are a few nouns which are 'syncopated'—that is, ε between a dental and ρ is dropped, a syllable being thus lost. They present no real difficulty, but, by reason of the importance and frequent occurrence of one of them, it will be well to give its paradigm in full.

πατήρ = father; stem—πατερ

	Singular	*Plural*
N.	πατήρ	πατέρες
A.	πατέρα	πατέρας
G.	πατρός	πατέρων
D.	πατρί	πατράσι

77. *Model* **c.** There is one model which needs to be carefully distinguished from both **a** (para. 75) and **b** (para. 76). The nom. sing. appears to be identical with such forms as αἰών and ποιμήν, but the stem ends in ντ, preceded by a short vowel. Now, inasmuch as ν, ρ, and ς (ξ, ψ) are the only three consonants which can end a purely Greek word, the τ is, in this model, dropped (cp. model **d**, para. 78), but the loss is compensated for by lengthening the preceding vowel.

λέων (m.) = lion; stem—λεοντ

	Singular	*Plural*
N.	λέων	λέοντες
A.	λέοντα	λέοντας
G.	λέοντος	λεόντων
D.	λέοντι	λέουσι

The same process of compensation takes place in dat. pl.,

such a cacophonous collocation of consonants as ντσ being quite impossible in Greek, which strives always for beauty of sound, or euphony; hence λέοντσι becomes λέουσι.

78. Model d. There is a large class of nouns, all neuter, of the 3rd decl. ending in the nom. sing. in μα, the stem ending in ματ. These are to be distinguished from fem. nouns of the 1st decl. in α (para. 18 (*b*) and (*c*)).

σῶμα = body; stem—σωματ

	Singular	*Plural*
N., A.	σῶμα	σώματα
G.	σώματος	σωμάτων
D.	σώματι	σώμασι

In the dat. pl. τ is dropped before σι, and also in the nom. sing., as no Greek word can end in τ.

79. Model e. Very many nouns add ς to the stem, with or without modification thereof. If the stem ends in a guttural, the addition of the ς makes the double letter ξ (κηρυκ-, κῆρυξ, m., herald); if in a labial, ψ results (λαιλαπ-, λαῖλαψ, f., storm); if in a dental, that letter is dropped (λαμπαδ-, λαμπάς, f., lamp). Such a word as πούς, m., foot, is not irregular, inasmuch as its stem is ποδ, and the ο is lengthened to ου by way of compensation for the loss of the δ. So also οὖς, n., ear; stem—ὠτ.

80. Model f. We have had (para. 75) one model (**a**) in which the stem ends in a consonant, and remains unchanged; there is a model in which the stem ends in a vowel (**v**), and is unchanged.

ἰχθύς (m.) = fish; stem—ἰχθυ

	Singular	Plural
N.	ἰχθύς	ἰχθύες
A.	ἰχθύν	ἰχθύας
G.	ἰχθύος	ἰχθύων
D.	ἰχθύϊ	ἰχθύσι

Here, it will be seen, the acc. sing. adds ν to the stem, whereas in model (a) α was added; otherwise the declension of these two models is the same. Cp. also model g (para. 81).

81. Model g. Yet another subdivision of this declension is that of nouns ending in ις. These are feminine. For the nom. sing. ς is added to the unaltered stem; but in some of the other cases the ι is changed into ε, with or without contraction. In the gen. sing. we find the ending ως instead of ος. As the stem ends in a vowel, the acc. sing. is formed by adding ν.

πόλις = city; stem—πολι

	Singular	Plural
N.	πόλις	πόλ|εες = εις
A.	πόλιν	πόλ|εας = εις
G.	πόλεως	πόλεων
D.	πόλ|έϊ = ει	πόλεσι

82. Model h. A fairly large class of nouns of this declension end in the nom. sing. in εύς. These are masculine. The declension may seem somewhat irregular, but it is not so in reality: the υ represents an old Greek letter, *digamma* (= Ϝ), and this is dropped before vowels, with or without resulting contraction.

βασιλεύς = king; stem—βασιλεϜ

	Singular	Plural
N.	βασιλεύς	βασιλ|έες = εῖς
A.	βασιλέα	βασιλέας
G.	βασιλέως	βασιλέων
D.	βασιλ|έϊ = εῖ	βασιλεῦσι

Notice here also what is known as the 'Attic' ending ως in the gen. sing. (cp. model (g), para. 81).

83. *Model* **i.** It was remarked in para. 33 that there are neuter nouns of the 3rd decl. whose nominative ends in ος, to be distinguished from masc. and fem. nouns of the 2nd decl. with the same ending; these may now be taken.   The important point in them is that the final letter of the stem (ς) is in some cases dropped between two vowels, and that contraction then takes place.   There are quite a number of such nouns, and they are all declined alike, thus:

$$\gamma\acute{\epsilon}\nu os = \text{race, kindred; stem} — \gamma\epsilon\nu\epsilon s$$

	Singular	*Plural*
N., A.	γένος	γέν|εσα = εα = η
G.	γέν|εσος = εος = ους	γεν|εσων = έων = ῶν
D.	γέν|εσι = ει	γένεσι

The variations in these nouns from those of model (a) (para. 75) are in appearance only.   The gen. sing. is still to be regarded as ending in ος (para. 74), though this is obscured by the contraction of ε and ο into ου.   The nom. pl., being neut., still ends in α (para. 17 (iii)), though, again, ε + α = η.

84. No further models need be given, as all nouns belonging to the 3rd decl. may be understood in the light of these nine. It may again be repeated that they all conform to the general type given in para. 74, and what may be termed the 'family likeness' should be recognized.

CLASSIFICATION OF NOUNS

85. The following table may prove helpful in dealing with nouns in so far as they are classifiable from the standpoint of nom. sing. termination and gender.   With it we take leave of nouns, except for those which are irregular or variable.

Decl.	M.	F.	N.
1st	ας, ης	α, η	none
2nd	ος	ος	ον
3rd	εύς	ις	μα
	ων		ος

VOCABULARIES

86. *Neuter Nouns of the 3rd Decl. ending in* μα (model (**d**)): αἷμα, blood; γράμμα, letter (of the alphabet); δικαίωμα, ordinance, statute; δόγμα, decree; κλῆμα, branch (of a vine only); ὄνομα, name; πλήρωμα, fullness; πνεῦμα, wind, spirit; πολίτευμα, commonwealth; στίγμα, mark, brand; στόμα, mouth.

87. *Feminine Nouns of the 3rd Decl. ending in* ις (model (**g**)): ἀνάμνησις, remembrance; ἀνάστασις, resurrection, rising up *or* again; ἀπόκρισις, answer; γνῶσις, knowledge; δύναμις, power; κλῆσις, calling; κρίσις, judgement; πίστις, faith.

88. *Neuter Nouns of the 3rd Decl. ending in* ος (model (**i**)): εἶδος, form; ἔθνος, nation; ἔτος, year; μέλος, limb, member of the body; μέρος, part; ὄρος, mountain; σκεῦος, vessel; τέλος, end.

89. διά, c. gen., through, by means of; c. acc., because of, on account of; χωρίς (c. gen.), without; νεκρός, ά, όν, dead.

Idiomatic Expressions

90. διὰ τοῦτο, on-account-of this = therefore; εἰς τὸν αἰῶνα, unto the age = for ever; εἰς τὸν αἰῶνα τοῦ αἰῶνος, unto the age of the age (also εἰς τοὺς αἰῶνας τῶν αἰώνων, unto the ages of the ages, etc.) = for ever and ever.

IRREGULAR NOUNS

91. ἀνήρ (**b**), stem ἀνερ, but δ is substituted for the ε for the sake of euphony—see para. 14, man, husband (Lat. *vir*, Ger. *Mann*; contrast ἄνθρωπος, para. 26).

γάλα (n., (**d**), stem γαλακτ), milk.
γυνή ((**d**), stem γυναικ, voc. γυναί), woman, wife.
θρίξ (f., (**e**), stem τριχ, dat. pl. θριξί), hair.
κύων (m., (**a**), stem κυν), dog.
μάρτυς (m., (**e**), stem μαρτυρ), witness.
νύξ (f., (**e**), stem νυκτ), night.

EXERCISE 6

A. Turn into Greek:

These are sons of God. The holy one of God. The bodies of the saints. The church is the body of Christ. Christ is the head of the church. By (ἐν) the Spirit of God. The same Spirit. I am not a slave of the letter.

B. Give English for:

τὸ ἡμῶν πολίτευμα ἐν τοῖς οὐρανοῖς ἐστιν. τὸ πνεῦμα τοῦ Θεοῦ τὸ ἅγιον. αὐτοὶ ὑμεῖς κλήματα τῆς ἀμπέλου τῆς οὐρανίου ἐστέ. τὸ ὄνομά μου Ἀνδρέας ἐστιν. οἱ λόγοι τοῦ στόματος αὐτοῦ ἀγαθοὶ ἦσαν. τὸ αἷμα Ἰησοῦ Χριστοῦ τοῦ υἱοῦ τοῦ Θεοῦ. γράμματα μεγάλα ἐν τῇ βίβλῳ ταύτῃ ἐστι. αὐτὸ τὸ πνεῦμα. τίνος τοῦτο τὸ δόγμα;

NUMERALS

92. These are really adjectives (para. 50), inasmuch as they modify nouns. They are—*cardinal*, denoting how many, or *ordinal*, denoting sequence. Of the former, the first four are declined, partly or wholly; the hundreds are declined (in the pl.) like qualifying adjectives of the first form (para. 51); and all, in so far as they are declined, conform, of course, to Rule 7 (para. 53). All ordinals are declined like qualifying adjectives of the first form (para. 51).

εἷς, one	πρῶτος, η, ον, first
δύο, two	δεύτερος, second
τρεῖς, three	τρίτος, third
τέσσαρες, four	τέταρτος, fourth
πέντε, five	πέμπτος, fifth
ἕξ, six	ἕκτος, sixth
ἑπτά, seven	ἕβδομος, seventh
ὀκτώ, eight	ὄγδοος, eighth
ἐννέα, nine	ἔνατος, ninth
δέκα, ten	δέκατος, tenth
ἕνδεκα, eleven	ἐνδέκατος, eleventh
δώδεκα, twelve	δωδέκατος, twelfth

93. 'One' is declined throughout:

	M.	F.	N.
N.	εἷς	μία	ἕν
A.	ἕνα	μίαν	ἕν
G.	ἑνός	μιᾶς	ἑνός
D.	ἑνί	μιᾷ	ἑνί

The fem. follows model (**c**) of the 1st decl. (para. 18); the masc. and neut. are of the 3rd decl.—cp. τις (para. 74). The numeral 'one' is sometimes used in the sense of our 'a' or 'an'; this is our own usage really, since 'an' is a form of 'one', and 'a', again, simply 'an' with the *n* dropped before a consonant or accented aspirate.

Example:

| ἰδὼν | συκῆν | μίαν | (Mat. 21. 19) |
| seeing | fig-tree | one | |

A numeral commonly follows the noun.

94. There are negative compounds of all three genders of the numeral 'one' (see para. 93): οὐδείς, οὐδεμία, οὐδέν; μηδείς, μηδεμία, μηδέν. These are declined exactly like their positive counterparts, and their meaning is obvious—no man *or* no one, no woman, nothing; bearing in mind, however, that it is a question of the gender of words, and not necessarily of things or persons. If resolved into their components (οὐδὲ εἷς, etc.) they are more emphatic—not even one. The alternative forms, with οὐ and μή, are connected with the general distinction between these two negative particles.

95. There is a dat. only of δύο: δυσί(ν).

96. τρεῖς is declined thus: neut. nom. and acc., τρία; gen., all genders, τριῶν; dat., all genders, τρισί(ν); there is only the one form for the masc. and fem. nom. and acc.

97. τέσσαρες, or τέσσερες, is thus declined: in the fem. the nom. is the same as in the masc.; the neut. nom. and acc. is τέσσαρα; masc. and fem. acc., τέσσαρας; gen., all genders, τεσσάρων; dat., all genders, τέσσαρσι(ν).

EXERCISE 7

A. Translate:

μεγάλη σου ἡ πίστις. οἱ δώδεκα σὺν Ἰησοῦ ἦσαν ἐν πόλει τινί. σὺ μετ’ ἐμοῦ εἶ. δύο υἱοὶ ἀνθρώπῳ τινι ἦσαν. τῆς βασιλείας αὐτοῦ οὐκ ἔσται τέλος. τὸ σῶμα χωρὶς πνεύματος νεκρόν ἐστιν. τῇ πρώτῃ ἡμέρᾳ τοῦ ἔτους (simple dat. = in *or* on).

B. Give Greek for:

Many are the vessels of the temple. There are seven mountains in the eternal city. We are members of the body of *the* Christ. The resurrection of the dead. O great mountain! The ordinances of God came through the mouth of his prophets. (In) the same year. *The* faith without works is dead.

QUALIFYING ADJECTIVES
Second Form

98. These follow the 1st decl. for the fem. and the 3rd for the masc. and neut.   There are three types.   It is unnecessary to set out the fem., because it is quite regular and always ends in α (see paras. 18 (*b*) and (*c*)).

Type 1: ὀξύς, ὀξεῖα, ὀξύ, sharp

	Singular		Plural	
	M.	N.	M.	N.
N.	ὀξύς	ὀξύ	ὀξεῖς	ὀξέα(ῆ)
A.	ὀξύν	ὀξύ	ὀξεῖς	ὀξέα(ῆ)
G.	ὀξέως		ὀξέων	
D.	ὀξεῖ		ὀξέσι	

Type 2: πᾶς, πᾶσα, πᾶν, all every

	M.	N.	M.	N.
N.	πᾶς	πᾶν	πάντες	πάντα
A.	πάντα	πᾶν	πάντας	πάντα
G.	πάντος		πάντων	
D.	πάντι		πᾶσι	

ἅπας, rather a literary word, and used for preference after consonants, is declined in exactly the same way.

Type 3: ἑκών, ἑκοῦσα, ἑκόν, willing

	M.	N.	M.	N.
N.	ἑκών	ἑκόν	ἑκόντες	ἑκόντα
A.	ἑκόντα	ἑκόν	ἑκόντας	ἑκόντα
G.	ἑκόντος		ἑκόντων	
D.	ἑκόντι		ἑκοῦσι	

It will be observed that—

in type 1, masculines and neuters combine models **g** and **i,**

in type 2, the masc. roughly follows model **e** and the
neut. model **c**,

in type 3, both genders follow model **e**,

always allowing for the general rules (para. 17 (iii)) regarding
neuters. ἄκων (unwilling) is declined similarly, and these are
the only adjs. of this type in N.T.

Type 2 is an exact model for aor. act. parts. (-σας, -σασα,
-σαν), and type 3 for pres. and fut. act. parts. (-ων, -ουσα, -ον);
see paras. 141, 142.

Πᾶς is naturally of frequent occurrence. It may or may not
take the def. art. Sometimes a distinction is to be observed in
this respect, at others it does not seem to matter whether the
art. is used or not: πᾶσα πόλις = every city, πᾶσα ἡ πόλις = all
the city *or* the whole city. Allowance must always be made
for the differing modes of expression in Greek and English:
we cannot say 'every wisdom', but 'all wisdom' (πᾶσα σοφία);
πᾶσα γῆ *or* πᾶσα ἡ γῆ = the whole earth (*or* land) *or* all the
earth.

A common phrase is such a one as πᾶς ὁ πιστεύων (John
3. 16, etc.) = everyone who believes *or* every believer; here,
however, the omission of the art. would modify the meaning—
'everyone, believing'. Τὰ πάντα = the universe. Moulton
translates πάντα ταῦτα 'all these things', ταῦτα πάντα 'these
things, all taken together'; but this is not a difference of
meaning, only of emphasis, and a very fine one!

EXERCISE 8

A. Give English for:

ἐγώ εἰμι ὁ ποιμὴν ὁ καλός. φονεύς ἐστι. μετὰ τρία ἔτη.
τὰ δέκα κέρατα καὶ αἱ ἑπτὰ κεφαλαὶ τοῦ θηρίου. πολλοὶ
ἱερεῖς σὺν τῷ βασιλεῖ. δώδεκα μῆνες ἐν ἔτει εἰσιν. διὰ τοῦτο
οὐδεὶς τῶν γραμματέων ἐκείνων μετ' ἐμοῦ ἐν τῇ ἐμῇ βασιλείᾳ
ἔσται. ταῦτα τὰ μεγάλα τέρατα ἔσονται ἐν οὐρανῷ.

B. Turn into Greek:

The child's parents are not in the holy city. God is our Saviour. This man is the great power of God. This God will be our God for ever. The good knowledge of God. The nations of the earth are many. In the twelfth month of the year. Many blind men are in the way. There shall be one shepherd.

VOCABULARIES

99. *Nouns of the 3rd decl.*: ἄρχων (c), ruler, leader, prince; δάκρυ (n. (f), δακρυ), tear; ἐλπίς (f. (e), ἐλπιδ), hope; θέλημα, will; θυγάτηρ (b), daughter; κεντυρίων (a), centurion; μήτηρ (b), mother; ὄρνις (m.-f. (e), ὀρνιθ), bird; ὄφις (m. (g)), serpent; οὖς (n. (e), ὠτ), ear; παῖς (m.-f. (e), παιδ), child, boy or girl; πῦρ (n. (a)), fire; σάρξ (f. (e), σαρκ), flesh; χάρις (f., (e) χαριτ), grace; χειμών (a), winter.

100. *Other Nouns:* μονή, dwelling-place, room; ἄρτος (m.), bread, a loaf; γεωργός, husbandman.

101. *Qualifying Adjectives, First Form:* ἀληθινός, ή, όν, real, true, genuine; σκληρός, ά, όν, hard.

EXERCISE 9

A. Give English for:

ἡ κρίσις ἡ ἐμὴ δικαία ἐστι. τοῦτό ἐστιν τὸ θέλημα τοῦ πατρός μου. ἐγώ εἰμι ὁ ἄρτος τῆς ζωῆς. σκληρός ἐστιν ὁ λόγος οὗτος. ἐγώ εἰμι τὸ φῶς τοῦ κόσμου. σὺ μαθητὴς εἶ ἐκείνου. ἐν ἐμοὶ ὁ πατήρ ἐστι κἀγὼ ἐν τῷ πατρί. ἐν τῇ οἰκίᾳ τοῦ πατρός μου μοναὶ πολλαί εἰσιν. ἐγώ εἰμι ἡ ἄμπελος ἡ ἀληθινή, καὶ ὁ πατήρ μου ὁ γεωργός ἐστιν. ἐξ αὐτοῦ καὶ δι᾽ αὐτοῦ καὶ εἰς αὐτὸν τὰ πάντα· αὐτῷ ἡ δόξα εἰς τοὺς αἰῶνας. οὗτοι οἱ λόγοι πιστοὶ καὶ ἀληθινοί.

B. Render into Greek:

There are men, women, and children in this city. These words are hard. All things are *out* of God. Peace [be] to you. The birds of *the* heaven are many. The Wicked One is the prince of this world. In God's will is our peace. *The* faith, *the* hope, and *the* love.

QUALIFYING ADJECTIVES
Third Form

102. These follow the 3rd decl. of nouns. The only distinction of gender is that the neut. nom.—and therefore the acc.—in both numbers has a form of its own; in the sing. this is the unaltered stem, while in the masc.-fem. the stem is modified. Two types may be given.

Type 1: σώφρων, sober-minded

	Singular		*Plural*	
	M. and F.	**N.**	**M. and F.**	**N.**
N.	σώφρων	σῶφρον	σώφρονες	σώφρονα
A.	σώφρονα	σῶφρον	σώφρονας	σώφρονα
G.	σώφρονος		σωφρόνων	
D.	σώφρονι		σώφροσι	

Taking nouns and adjectives together, it will be seen that a nom. termination ων may be from a stem ending in ων (para. 75), οντ (para. 77), or ον, as here; the stem is shown by the gen. sing., as given in lexicons, and care is needed to avoid confusion.

Type 2: ἀληθής, true

N.	ἀληθής	ἀληθές	ἀληθεῖς	ἀληθῆ
A.	ἀληθῆ	ἀληθές	ἀληθεῖς	ἀληθῆ
G.	ἀληθοῦς		ἀληθῶν	
D.	ἀληθεῖ		ἀληθέσι	

For the contractions, cp. paras. 82 and 83.   This concludes the declension of adjectives.

103. Rule 9.   *The neuter form of an adjective may be used adverbially*—e.g., μόνος = alone, μόνον = only; πρῶτος = first, πρῶτον = firstly, in the first place.

COMPARISON OF ADJECTIVES

104.   Most qualifying adjectives are capable of expressing three degrees of the quality indicated, known as *positive*, *comparative*, and *superlative*.   The first simply states; the second expresses a higher degree, as compared with another person or thing; the third expresses the highest degree of all, either relatively to all other persons or things, or absolutely in itself.   In English—

Pos.	strong
Comp.	stronger
Sup. { relative . . .	strongest
{ absolute . . .	most strong, very strong

We are to see how Greek manipulates its adjectives in this respect.   It does so in two ways.

First Form

105.   Here the following endings are added to the stem of the positive form, and the resulting word is declined like a first-form qualifying adjective (para. 51):

Comp.	τερος, τέρα, τερον
Sup.	τατος, τάτη, τατον

Note that Greek has only one way of expressing the superlative relative and absolute.   Thus—

> ἰσχυρός, ά, όν, strong, powerful
> ἰσχυρότερος, α, ον, stronger, more powerful
> ἰσχυρότατος, η, ον, strongest, most (very) strong

As a mnemonic aid, it may be observed that, in the comparative, the syllable *er* in the English suggests the ερ of the Greek.

If the stem-ending o, in adjectives of the first form, is preceded by a short syllable, the o is lengthened to ω in the comp. and sup. Thus—

νέος, α, ον, new
νεώτερος, α, ον, newer (*also* younger)
νεώτατος, η, ον, newest, youngest

Second Form

106. Here (a small class) the following endings are added to the adjective stem, perhaps modified:

Comp. . . . . ίων (m.-f.), ιον
Sup. . . . . . ιστος, η, ον

The comp. in this form is declined like σώφρων (para. 102), but the sup. like first-form qualifying adjectives. Thus—

ταχύς, εῖα, ύ, swift
ταχίων, ιον, swifter
τάχιστος, η, ον, swiftest, most (very) swift

Irregular Forms

107. As in English, etc., some common adjectives are compared irregularly. Thus—

ἀγαθός, good, βελτίων or κρείσσων, better, βέλτιστος or κράτιστος, best
κάκος, bad, κακίων or χείρων, worse, κάκιστος or χείριστος, worst
μικρός, little, ἐλάσσ(ττ)ων, smaller, less, ἐλάχιστος, smallest, least
πολύς, much, great, πλείων or πλέων, more, πλεῖστος, most
μέγας, great, μείζων or μειζότερος, greater, μέγιστος, greatest

In addition, μικρός forms μικρότερος; and ἥσσων *or* ἥττων may mean 'less' or 'worse'. Some of these forms, it will be seen, are partly regular, and in others the variations from the normal are due to the demands of euphony.

108. There is one very interesting form, to which special attention may be directed in passing. The apostle Paul, in Eph. 3. 8, to express his sense of personal unworthiness, coins a word—ἐλαχιστότερος. Now, as ἐλάχιστος is already a superlative, Paul's word can only mean 'leaster'! A.V. happily gives 'less than the least'.

THE CONSTRUCTION OF COMPARATIVES

109. Greek has various ways of constructing a sentence so as to express comparison between one person or thing and another —two, (*a*) and (*b*), in particular.

(*a*) The objects compared may be connected by ἤ = (than, or) (note accent and breathing), which takes the same case after it as before.

Example:

Ἰησοῦς πλείονας μαθητὰς ποιεῖ καὶ βαπτίζει ἤ Ἰωάννης (John 4. 1)
= Jesus is making and baptizing more disciples than John

(*b*) That with which comparison is made may be put in the genitive case, the connective 'than' being then suppressed.

Examples:

ὁ πατήρ μου πάντων μεῖζόν ἐστιν (John 10. 29)
= my Father is greater than all
ἔστιν ἀπίστου χείρων (I Tim. 5. 8)
= he is worse than an unbeliever

ἤ is commonly, but not invariably, used after μᾶλλον (rather) where whole clauses are concerned.

Example:

ὑμῶν ἀκούειν μᾶλλον ἢ τοῦ Θεοῦ (Acts 4. 19)
= to hear you rather than God

Θεοῦ is gen., not because it is the object of comparison, but
because, like ὑμῶν, it is governed by the verb ἀκούειν.

(c) ὑπέρ may be used to heighten the comparison.

Example:

οἱ υἱοὶ τοῦ αἰῶνος τούτου φρονιμώτεροι ὑπὲρ τοὺς υἱοὺς
τοῦ φωτὸς εἰς τὴν γενεὰν τὴν ἑαυτῶν εἰσίν (Luke 16. 8)
= the sons of this age are more prudent beyond the sons
of light in their generation

(d) παρά also is found thus used.

Example:

κρείττοσι θυσίαις παρὰ ταύτας (Heb. 9. 23)
= with better sacrifices beside these

A wide variety of phrasing is found in comparisons, and care
and judgement must be exercised in construing, especially
where the neuter of an adjective is used adverbially; but the
above will put the student on the track to be followed.

VOCABULARY

Adjectives and Their Comparatives

110. μακάρι|ος, α, ον, happy, blessed—ώτερος; σοφ|ός, ή, όν,
wise—ώτερος; ἀσθεν|ής, ές, weak—έστερος; φρόνιμ|ος, ον,
prudent—ώτερος.

EXERCISE 10

A. Give English for:

οὐκ ἔστιν δοῦλος μείζων τοῦ κυρίου αὐτοῦ. ἡμεῖς μάρτυρές
ἐσμεν τούτων. παῖδες οὔκ εἰσι μοί. ἐγὼ ὁ Θεὸς τῶν πατέρων

σου. αὐτὴ νεωτέρα ἐστιν ἢ αὐτῆς ἡ ἀδελφή. τὸ ἀσθενὲς τοῦ
Θεοῦ ἰσχυρότερον τῶν ἀνθρώπων. οἱ υἱοὶ τοῦ αἰῶνος τούτου
φρονιμώτεροι τῶν υἱῶν τοῦ φωτός.

B. Render into Greek:

God is stronger than we [are]. The priests are most wise.
Therefore the sons of God are happier than the sons of this
world. They are very prudent. Peace [be] to this house.

THE CONJUGATION OF THE VERB
(Read paras. 14, 15)

111. No part of our course will call for closer application—
but, by way of recompence, none will be found of greater
interest—than the verb. The Greek verb is distinguished by
fullness and flexibility. True to the synthetic nature of the
language, from a stem giving the bare idea of the verb the
various modifications thereof are made by the addition of
terminations and otherwise, generally within the limits of a
single word. If the instruction now to be given is carefully
followed, learners will find their path to the complete mastery
of the Greek verb made as free from difficulty as possible.

112. A verb is conjugated for five things—voice, mood, tense,
person, and number; and these have to be considered in every
verb form.

The VOICE indicates whether the subject performs the action
—physical or mental—with reference to someone or something
else (*active* voice), or the action returns to himself (*middle*),
or he himself is the object of another's action (*passive*).

The MOOD, as the word implies, shows the state of mind of
the subject—the 'mood' he is in; or it may be said to be a
'mode' of speaking. If he makes an affirmation—positively
or negatively—he uses the *indicative* mood; if he issues a
command or prohibition, the *imperative* (but see later); if he

makes a supposition of any kind, the *subjunctive* or *optative*. There are also the *participles* and the *infinitive*—often wrongly called moods.

The TENSE is of course either *past*, *present*, or *future*, though these are not the actual terms used, as will be seen.

The PERSON is either 1st (I—we), 2nd (thou—ye), or 3rd (he, she, *or* it—they).

The NUMBER is, as just shown, *singular* or *plural*, there being no dual in N.T.

113. Before any terminations are given at length, the following table is introduced—as a map of the main features of an unknown country is a preparation for the study of topographical details. Everyone is familiar with the above threefold division of time into past, present, or future. It is necessary to think also of an action as being either *indefinite* or *momentary* ('punctiliar' is also used), *continuous* (or 'linear'), or *complete* or perfect; and as any one such kind of action may take place at any time a perfect verb-system should provide for nine 'tenses'. Of this possible nine, Greek has in fact seven, or, confining ourselves to N.T., six. No more suitable word can be chosen to exemplify these than πιστεύω = I believe; for one thing, it is absolutely regular, and, for another, it occurs very frequently, being, indeed, one of the characteristic terms of the Christian faith. Moreover, this verb is typical of a large class (A 1) conjugated identically. In it, and in all those with which we are concerned until further notice, the 1st pers. sing. pres. ind. act. ends in ω; and this applies to the overwhelming majority of Greek verbs as found in N.T., which are therefore said to belong to the ω conj. This is also known as the 1st conj., being taken first in study; the 2nd or μι conj., really the older of the two, will be dealt with later (only some three dozen verbs).

114.

TABLE OF TENSE-FORMS—ACTIVE VOICE, INDICATIVE MOOD

	INDEFINITE	CONTINUOUS	COMPLETE
PRESENT	— (I believe) —	πιστεύ-ω I am believing *Present*	πε-πίστευ-κα I have believed *Present-Perfect*
PAST	ἐ-πίστευ-σ-α I believed *Aorist*	ἐ-πίστευ-ον I was believing *Imperfect*	ἐ-πε-πιστεύ-κειν I had believed *Past-Perfect*
FUTURE	πιστεύ-σ-ω I shall believe *Future*	— (I shall be believing) —	— (I shall have believed) —

115. *Remarks and Explanations:*

(*a*) In practice, the present indefinite is supplied by the form for the continuous, so that πιστεύω means 'I believe' as well as 'I am believing', and our emphatic 'I do believe' in addition. Conversely, the future continuous is supplied by the indefinite.

(*b*) As in the verb 'to be' (paras. 39–41), the pronoun subject (nom.) is not expressed unless it is meant to be emphatic; the terminations convey the idea of the person—1st, 2nd, or 3rd, sing. or pl.

(*c*) The stem πιστευ will be seen to remain unaltered throughout, and this is so with all verbs the stem of which ends in ευ, and of nearly all in a close vowel (ι or υ).

(*d*) In the three past-time forms it will be noted that the vowel ἐ is prefixed; this is called the 'augment', and is the sign of past time in the indicative mood only. This ἐ is thus prefixed when the verb begins with a consonant, and is then known as the 'syllabic augment', because it forms an additional syllable; when the verb begins with a vowel this procedure is modified, as will be unfolded in due course.

(e) The sign of completed action, in all moods (not only the indicative), is the prefixing to the stem of a syllable consisting of the initial consonant and ε. In conjugating δουλεύω (I serve), therefore, the prefixed syllable is δε; and so on. This is called the 'reduplication'. If a verb begins with an aspirated consonant (χ, φ, or θ) the corresponding sharp (κ, π, τ—see para. 10) is used for this purpose; thus, in conjugating φονεύω (I kill, murder) πε is the reduplication; in θεραπεύω (I cure, attend), τε. This reduplication is not always carried out when the verb begins with σ, but the augment only is used.

(f) Hence it arises that the form expressing completed action in past time has both reduplication and augment—ἐπεπιστεύκειν; this again, however, is not always consistently carried out.

(g) The last line in each division of the table, in italic, is the name by which that particular form will be called in this Primer.

(h) The only difference between the present and the future is the addition of σ to the stem for the latter, with the same terminations as for the former, and this will be found to be always the relation between these two tenses in the active and middle voices; knowing one, therefore, the other follows, with allowance for the laws of euphony in other classes of verbs.

(i) Only one instance occurs in T.R. (Luke 19. 40) of the future-perfect, and as this is not admitted by Nestle and others it is ignored here.

(j) One precautionary word. No more fruitful cause of misunderstanding the Greek verb system exists than the assumption that, because the aorist indicative is a past-tense form, therefore 'aorist' connotes past time; but this is not so. The term comes from α (the privative or negative α, = Lat. un-, in-) and ὁρίζω (I mark out or define; cp. our word 'horizon'), and means, therefore, 'undefined', 'indefinite'.

The aorist indicative is a past-tense form, but it is the augment, the sign of past time, which makes it so, not the term 'aorist'. In other moods it is not a past form at all, but simply 'punctiliar'—that is, denoting action at a point in time, rather than a continuous process, for which the term 'present' is reserved. An aorist participle may refer to future time if the context demands.

(k) Verbs generally have their accent as far back as possible; exceptions will be noted.

116.

SYNOPSIS OF TERMINATIONS—ACTIVE VOICE, INDICATIVE MOOD

Present:

ω	εις	ει	ομεν	ετε	ουσι

Imperfect (with augment—see para. 115 (d)):

ον	ες	ε	ομεν	ετε	ον

Aorist (with augment):

σα	σας	σε(ν)	σαμεν	σατε	σαν

Future (cp. Present):

σω	σεις	σει	σομεν	σετε	σουσι

Present-Perfect (with reduplication—see para. 115 (e)):

κα	κας	κε(ν)	καμεν	κατε	κασι

Past-Perfect (with augment and reduplication—see para. 115 (f)):

κειν	κεις	κει	κειμεν	κειτε	κεισαν

These terminations, which should be studied as well as memorized, are simply added to verbal stems ending in ι or υ; and while they may not all occur in any one verb the various possible combinations should be formed for practice; thus— ἐπίστευσαν = they believed, πιστεύσει = he will believe.

117. The indicative is the *stating* mood, and all sentences coming under this description contain verbs in that mood. As in English, however, the fut. ind. may be used to express a command (see para. 112). This comes out especially in prohibitions, which are simply, in this usage, commands negatived by the use of οὐ.

Examples:

αὐτῷ μόνῳ λατρεύσεις (Mat. 4. 10)
= to him only thou shalt do service
οὐ μοιχεύσεις (Mat. 19. 18)
= thou shalt not commit adultery

This usage is extended to the pl.

118. A question is seen to be such by its punctuation, not by the order of the words or otherwise.

Example:

πιστεύεις τουτο; (John 11. 26)
= believest thou this?

119. Active verbs, when used transitively (that is, when the action 'passes over' to an object), govern cases (see para. 22). It may be taken that a verb takes the accusative unless otherwise laid down (verbs of mental emotion, such as πιστεύω, take the dative).

VOCABULARY

120. A 1 Verbs (para. 150): ἀπολύω, I dismiss; βασιλεύω, I reign; δακρύω, I shed tears, weep; δουλεύω (c. dat.), I serve (as a slave); θεραπεύω, I heal; θύω, I slay; λύω, I loose; μνημονεύω (c. gen.), I remember; νηστεύω, I fast; προφητεύω, I prophesy; φυτεύω, I plant; χρίω, I anoint ; σαλεύω, I shake.

EXERCISE 11

A. Give English for:

μνημονεύσομεν τῶν λογῶν τοῦ κυρίου Ἰησοῦ. πεφόνευκε ἄνθρωπον. ἀνήρ τις σεσάλευκε τὰς τοῦ ἱεροῦ θύρας. αἱ ἑπτὰ θυγάτερες αὐτοῦ ἐπροφήτευον. πάντες οἱ καλοὶ ἱερεῖς ἐνήστευον ἐν ταῖς ἡμεραῖς τοῦ νόμου. πιστεύομεν εἰς τὸν Θεὸν τὸν σωτῆρα πάντων ἀνθρώπων. οὐ ἐπίστευσαν πάντες ἐν τῷ Ἰησοῦ. σοὶ δουλεύσομεν, ὦ βασιλεῦ. ἐπεφύτευκει ἀμπελῶνα. προφητεύσουσιν ἐν ἐκείναις ταῖς ἡμεραῖς.

B. Render into Greek:

They will reign over (ἐπί, c. gen.) the earth. I will shake the heavens and the earth. He will cure my son. Dost thou believe (i.e., believest thou) *the* God? They are sacrificing to the true God. We do not fast in these days.

EXERCISE 12

A. Give English for:

ἐγὼ καὶ ὁ πατὴρ ἕν ἐσμεν. τούτῳ ἦσαν θυγατέρες τέσσαρες, καὶ ἐπροφήτευον. θεραπεύσω αὐτόν. ἐθεράπευσε τὸν ἄνθρωπον ὁ Ἰησοῦς. ἔχρισεν τὸν Ἰησοῦν τὸν ἀπὸ Ναζαρὲθ ὁ Θεὸς πνεύματι ἁγίῳ καὶ δυνάμει. δόξα τῷ πατρὶ καὶ τῷ υἱῷ καὶ τῷ πνεύματι τῷ ἁγίῳ. ἡ παῖς οὐκ ἔστι τυφλή. τὰ ὦτα τοῦ λέοντος μεγάλα, ἀλλὰ οἱ ὀδόντες τοῦ παιδὸς μικροί εἰσιν. ἐμνημόνευσαν οἱ μαθηταὶ τῶν λόγων Ἰησοῦ. ἦν ἡ μήτηρ τοῦ Ἰησοῦ ἐκεῖ. πεφύτευκα δένδρον ἐν τῷ κήπῳ αὐτοῦ οὗτος ὁ γεωργός.

B. Render into Greek:

We shall not fast at (in) that time (καιρός). The feet of the sheep are not large. I have healed her. I believe God. We believe in God the Father. Believe ye the Lord Jesus? We serve God with our spirit. I was fasting in the temple. We killed him. They did not believe his words. Ye serve the Lord Christ.

THE TENSES OF THE INDICATIVE

121. In addition to the general remarks and explanations
following the table of tenses (para. 115), a few lines may now
be devoted to making clear the force of these tenses, as used in
Greek, before turning to the other moods.

Present. Here, as already stated, the one form—continuous present—has to do duty for all English forms of the
present. Therefore the usual rendering is, for instance, 'I
believe', etc.; but sometimes the true force of the Greek is to
be recognized.

Example:

> Ἀρχέλαος βασιλεύει τῆς Ἰουδαίας ἀντὶ τοῦ πατρὸς αὐτοῦ
> (Mat. 2. 22)
> = Archelaus reigns (*or* is reigning) over Judæa instead of
> his father

Imperfect. This conveys the idea of action going on con-
tinuously in past time; what was habitual or customary.

Example:

> οὐδὲ γὰρ οἱ ἀδελφοὶ αὐτοῦ ἐπίστευον εἰς αὐτόν (John 7. 5)
> = for neither did his brethren believe in him

Aorist. This most precise tense speaks of action wholly in
past time, and sundered from the moment of speaking,
occupying either an instant or embracing a period. Our
English style will not always allow of this tense-form being
translated strictly, because the usages of any two languages do
not necessarily correspond (cp. the Fr. *l'homme que j'ai vu
hier* = the man whom I saw yesterday); but the force of the
Greek form should be felt by the student, and a careless
substitution of the English imperfect or present-perfect must
on no account be indulged in.

Example:

Διὰ τί οὖν οὐκ ἐπιστεύσατε αὐτῷ (Mat. 21. 25)
= Why then did ye not believe (*or* believed ye not) him?

John the Baptist was dead at the moment of speaking, and the question which the chief priests put into the mouth of Jesus relates wholly to the past.

Future. This tense needs no further elucidation (but see paras. 112 and 117).

Example:

τότε νηστεύσουσιν ἐν ἐκείναις ταῖς ἡμέραις (Luke 5. 35)
= then will they fast in those days

Present-Perfect. This, in distinction from the aorist, denotes past action continuing, or its effects remaining, down to the present—action in the past, indeed, but connected with the present, instead of separated from it; it must therefore commonly be rendered by an English present.

Example:

ἐγὼ πεπίστευκα ὅτι σὺ εἶ ὁ χριστός (John 11. 27)
= I have believed (= I believe) that thou art the Christ

Martha here affirms that at some time in the past she had exercised faith in the direction indicated, and that such was still, at the moment of speaking, her faith; hence the English present (cp. Paul's language in II Tim. 1. 12).

Past-Perfect. The same principle applies here, but the action continues down to a point in past time only, and so its equivalent is the English aorist.

Example:

παρέθεντο αὐτοὺς τῷ κυρίῳ εἰς ὃν πεπιστεύκεισαν
(Acts 14. 23)
= they commended them to the Lord, in whom they believed

Those referred to had at some previous point of time believed and at the moment referred to by the narrator were still exercising faith. Note the absence of the augment, the termination showing the tense (see para. 115 (f)).

122.

SYNOPSIS OF TERMINATIONS—ACTIVE VOICE, IMPERATIVE MOOD

Present:

| — | ϵ | $\acute{\epsilon}\tau\omega$ | — | $\epsilon\tau\epsilon$ | $\acute{\epsilon}\tau\omega\sigma\alpha\nu$ |

Aorist (without augment)*:*

| — | $\sigma o\nu$ | $\sigma\acute{a}\tau\omega$ | — | $\sigma a\tau\epsilon$ | $\sigma\acute{a}\tau\omega\sigma a\nu$ |

Perfect (with reduplication—see para. 115 (e))*:*

| — | $\kappa\epsilon$ | $\kappa\acute{\epsilon}\tau\omega$ | — | $\kappa\epsilon\tau\epsilon$ | $\kappa\acute{\epsilon}\tau\omega\sigma a\nu$ |

123. (*a*) The imperative is the *commanding* mood, and is the normal mood for commands, entreaties, exhortations, etc.; but see paras. 112, 117.

(*b*) There is of course no 1st pers., as one cannot command oneself to act, save in soliloquy, when one objectivizes oneself and speaks as though to the 2nd pers. sing.—for example, 'My soul, hope thou in God'.

(*c*) The English expression for the 3rd pers. is 'let him *or* them . . .'

(*d*) The notion of time is altogether absent, save that a command can obviously affect only future conduct; hence the disappearance of the augment. The present—unfortunately named; 'continuous' would undoubtedly be better—implies the continuance or repetition of the action commanded; the aor., on the contrary, refers to an isolated act only. The perf. is very rare, and connotes action complete in its results. The distinction between the two first especially is of great interest.

Examples:

πιστεύετε ἐν τῷ εὐαγγελίῳ (Mark 1. 15)
= believe ye in the gospel
Πίστευσον ἐπὶ τὸν κύριον Ἰησοῦν (Acts 16. 31)
= Believe thou on the Lord Jesus

(e) Negatived—always with μή, the hypothetical negative—a command becomes, of course, a prohibition. Here also the pres. and the aor. differ in their force; the former means 'cease what you are now doing', the latter 'do not commit such-and-such an action'.

Example:

Θυρατέρες Ἱερουσαλήμ, μὴ κλαίετε ἐπ' ἐμέ· πλὴν ἐφ' ἑαυτὰς κλαίετε καὶ ἐπὶ τὰ τέκνα ὑμῶν (Luke 23. 28)
= Daughters of Jerusalem, lament not (they were doing so—see verse 27) over me; but lament over yourselves and over your children

No suitable example occurs in N.T. of the aor. imperat. with μή; as a matter of fact, as will be seen, the aor. subj. is commonly used in this respect.

EXERCISE 13

A. Give English for:

λύσατε αὐτόν. ἀμπελῶνα ἄνθρωπος ἐφύτευσεν. μνημονεύετε ὑμεῖς τῶν ῥημάτων μου. πιστεύετε εἰς τὸν Θεόν, καὶ εἰς ἐμὲ πιστεύετε. μὴ κλαῖε, πίστευσον μόνον. οἱ Φαρισαῖοι ἐνήστευον. βασιλεύσει ἐπὶ τὸν οἶκον Ἰακὼβ εἰς τοὺς αἰῶνας, καὶ τῆς βασιλείας αὐτοῦ οὐκ ἔσται τέλος. ἀπόλυσον αὐτήν, ἐπιστάτα. ἐδάκρυσεν ὁ Ἰησοῦς.

B. Render into Greek:

Send the crowds away, Lord. Prophesy, King of the Jews. The sons of *the* Zebedee fasted on that day. Believe ye not me? Let them fast. Let him not lament. Remembered ye not my sayings? Heal me, O Lord. I have anointed my son. Shut the door.

SYNOPSIS OF TERMINATIONS—ACTIVE VOICE, SUBJUNCTIVE MOOD

124.

Present:

$$\omega \qquad \eta s \qquad \eta \qquad \omega\mu\epsilon\nu \qquad \eta\tau\epsilon \qquad \omega\sigma\iota(\nu)$$

Aorist (without augment):

$$\sigma\omega \qquad \sigma\eta s \qquad \sigma\eta \qquad \sigma\omega\mu\epsilon\nu \qquad \sigma\eta\tau\epsilon \qquad \sigma\omega\sigma\iota\nu$$

Perfect (with reduplication—see para. 115 (*e*)):

$$\kappa\omega \qquad \kappa\eta s \qquad \kappa\eta \qquad \kappa\omega\mu\epsilon\nu \qquad \kappa\eta\tau\epsilon \qquad \kappa\omega\sigma\iota\nu$$

These three 'tenses' are all there are in this mood. They are seen to be extremely simple in their formation and connection: the aor. is formed from the pres. by inserting σ between stem and termination, in exactly the same way as, in the ind. mood, the fut. was formed from the pres.; then the perf. is formed by the use of κ in the same way. Moreover, the pres. subj. terminations themselves differ from those of the ind. mood only in lengthening the vowel—$o\mu\epsilon\nu$ becoming $\omega\mu\epsilon\nu$, and so on, ι being subscript ($\epsilon\iota s$—ηs).

The word 'tense' is used for simplicity's sake. As a matter of fact—this has been already referred to—in moods other than the ind. we have to think of state rather than time; so here again, as in the imperat. mood (para. 123 (*d*)), it is a matter of continuous, momentary, or completed action respectively. Hence it is that the aor. has no augment, and there is but one perf.

125. The subjunctive is the *supposing* mood; it deals with possibilities, ideas, etc. (from the standpoint of the laws of human thought, of course), in contrast to the indicative, which deals with facts. In English, the mood is generally formed analytically (para. 14) with the auxiliary verb 'may'; but this is not to be taken as the necessary and invariable equivalent of the Greek. The mood is therefore to be looked for in 'dependent' sentences—that is, depending on a statement of fact (in the ind. mood) in the 'principal' sentence, and introduced by a suitable conjunction, such as ἵνα (= that, in order that).

Example:

οὗτος ἦλθεν εἰς μαρτυρίαν, ἵνα μαρτυρήσῃ περὶ τοῦ φωτός, ἵνα πάντες πιστεύσωσιν δι' αὐτοῦ (John 1. 7)

= he came for (the purpose of giving) testimony, in order that he might testify concerning the light, in order that all men might believe through him

Here we have first of all a statement of fact, and then two actions dependent on that fact, and both expressed in the subj. mood.

THE PROHIBITORY SUBJUNCTIVE

126. As previously stated (paras. 117 and 123) there is yet a third way of expressing a prohibition, and that is by the use of the aor. subj.

Example:

μὴ φονεύσῃς (James 2. 11)

= do not kill *or* murder

which, as will be recognized, is the same as—

οὐ φονεύσεις (Mat. 5. 20 *et al.*)

= thou shalt not kill

The former is the regular classical idiom, and is perhaps the stronger expression of the two.

THE HORTATORY SUBJUNCTIVE

127. It was pointed out in para. 123 (*b*) that there is no 1st pers. in the imperat. mood, because one cannot command oneself. There is, however, as there said, a familiar form of speech—'let us . . .'; and this is expressed by the 1st pers. plur. of the appropriate tense of the subj.

Example:

ἔχωμεν χάριν (Heb. 12. 28)
= let us hold fast grace
or, in the negative—
μὴ καθεύδωμεν ὡς οἱ λοιποί (I Thes. 5. 6)
= let us not sleep as [do] the rest

128. The negative with the subj. mood must always be μή (cp. para. 123 (*e*), and contrast with οὐ, para. 28). But both negative particles may be used together, with the aor. subj., to make an emphatic double negative, one strengthening the other, not, as in English, cancelling it.

Example:

οὐ μὴ πιστεύσητε (Luke 22. 67)
= ye will by no means believe

129. Rule 10. *Μή (and its compounds), introducing a question, is left untranslated, but suggests a negative answer.* This is a most interesting idiom, and its observance will yield interesting results.

Example:

Μήτι ἐγὼ ᾿Ιουδαῖός εἰμι; (John 18. 35)
= (A.V.) Am I a Jew?

Pilate was not asking for information, but spoke in scorn; his question amounted to—I am no Jew, am I?

A. Give English for:

μὴ κλαίωμεν. μὴ πιστεύσητε αὐτοῦ τοῖς λόγοις. μὴ
πίστευσα αὐτῷ; ὦ γυναί, μεγάλη ἡ πίστις σου. λαός ἐστί μοι
πολὺς ἐν τῇ πόλει ταύτῃ. ἀνδρὰς πολλοὺς ὁ Ἰησοῦς ἐθεράπευσε.
οὐ μὴ βασιλεύσῃς ἐπὶ τὸν λαόν μου. γυναῖκές τινες ἐπίστευσαν τῷ Ἰησοῦ. πιστεύομεν ἵνα δουλεύωμεν τῷ κυρίῳ.
χρῖσον αὐτὸν ἵνα προφητεύῃ. μὴ φονεύσωμεν αὐτούς.

B. Render into Greek:

Believe ye the gospel, that ye may have eternal life. Let us
not remember his evil words. Do we believe the saying?
[No.] Thou shalt by no means heal the man. Many women
were weeping in the city. The men did not shut the door.
Let us not serve the evil one. Let him plant the trees. I have
many things. Ye shall not fast. Let them not fast. Prophesy,
O man!

SYNOPSIS OF TERMINATIONS—ACTIVE VOICE, OPTATIVE MOOD

130.

Present:

| οιμι | οις | οι | οιμεν | οιτε | οιεν |

Aorist (without augment):

| σαιμι | σαις | σαι | σαιμεν | σαιτε | σαιεν |

The optative mood need not detain the student long at this
stage, but is given here for completeness' sake. It was falling
into disuse in the time of the writers of the N.T.; hence the
occurrence therein of the above two tenses only. Its terminations are characterized by diphthongal sounds; and these are
reckoned long here, not short, as in the nom. pl. of nouns,
so that, when final, they affect the accent.

The mood either expresses a wish, as its name implies (Lat.
opto = I wish), or has a potential meaning; but it is really a

division of the subjunctive mood, being the subjunctive of the historic tenses, and so is found in dependent sentences (see para. 125).

THE TEMPORAL AUGMENT

131. In para. 115 (*d*) it was said that when a verb begins with a vowel the syllabic augment cannot be prefixed as is done before a consonant. What then happens is that the initial vowel is lengthened, and this lengthened vowel is the 'temporal' augment, because it is the sign of past time in such verbs, but does not create an additional syllable. Of course, this concerns the indicative mood only, since only there is past time involved (imperf., aor., and past-perf.). The lengthening takes place thus: α becomes η; ε—η or ει; ι—ει; ο—ω; αι and ει—ῃ; αυ and ευ—ηυ; οι—ῳ. It will be seen that a ι in a diphthong is retained by becoming subscript; but when ι or υ stands alone as the initial syllable there may be nothing to show its augmentation except possibly a smooth breathing (') becoming rough ('). Long vowels and ου and some other diphthongs remain unchanged.

Example:

τοῦτον ἠγγάρευσαν (Mat. 27. 32)

= him they requisitioned

ἦν οἰκοδεσπότης ὅστις ᾠκοδόμησεν πύργον (Mat. 21. 33)

= there was a householder who built a tower.

IMPROPER REDUPLICATION

132. A further point is that as in such verbs the normal ε cannot be prefixed for past time, neither can the normal reduplication take place for completed action. In the perf., therefore, the temporal augment does duty also for the reduplication, which is then said to be 'improper'; it is continued right through the verb, in all moods, because it belongs as such to the perfect tenses. The termination, of course, will show whether in any

particular verb form one is confronted with a temporal augment
or an improper reduplication.

It therefore results that in looking in a lexicon for a verb of
which a past tense is known, allowance may have to be made
for the temporal augment or the improper reduplication as
may be.

NOTE. ἀκούω (I hear) is anomalous: aor. ind. ἤκουσα,
pres.-perf. ἀκήκοα.

RELATIVE PRONOUNS

133. In addition to the personal pronouns and the various
demonstrative adjectives used as such (paras. 36–38 and 62–67)
there are the relative pronouns—so called because they
'relate' to someone or something previously mentioned and
known as the 'antecedent'. The antecedent may, however, be
suppressed in Greek, where no ambiguity exists, as is done in
English in poetry or elevated prose—for example, 'Who steals
my purse steals trash' is elliptical for 'He, *or* the person, who,
etc.'

A clear understanding of the syntax of the relative is
necessary.

In 'The voice | which I heard | was loud' we have two distinct
sentences: (*a*) a *principal* sentence—'the voice was loud', and
(*b*) a subordinate (or *relative*) sentence, telling us what voice
was loud—'which I heard'. 'Which' is a relative pronoun,
and its antecedent is 'voice'. Such a sentence, answering the
question 'What?', is adjectival in force, and is called by the
Joint Committee on Grammatical Terminology an 'adjective
clause'. An important rule comes in here, which may be
formulated thus:

134. Rule 11.   *A relative pronoun must agree with its antecedent
in gender and number, but its case is determined by its function
in its own sentence.*

Thus, in the complex sentence above, 'voice' is fem. sing. in Greek, hence the rel. pron. must be so; but whereas 'voice' is the *subject* of the verb 'was', and therefore nom., 'which' is the *object* of the verb 'heard', and therefore acc. or gen. The sentence will therefore be ἡ φωνὴ | ἣν ἤκουσα | μεγάλη ἦν, if keeping to that order of words.

135. The rel. pron. is declined thus. It follows the def. art., but is aspirated throughout.

	Singular			*Plural*		
	M.	F.	N.	M.	F.	N.
N.	ὅς	ἥ	ὅ	οἵ	αἵ	ἅ
A.	ὅν	ἥν	ὅ	οὕς	ἅς	ἅ
G.	οὗ	ἧς	οὗ	ὧν	ὧν	ὧν
D.	ᾧ	ᾗ	ᾧ	οἷς	αἷς	οἷς

The rel. pron. enters into one or two idiomatic phrases—*e.g.*, ἀφ'οὗ or ἧς (cp. para. 12 (*a*)) = since. ὅς ἄν means 'whoever'. ὅ ἐστιν can introduce relative clauses containing interpretations, whatever be the gender and number of the antecedent.

In addition to the suppression of the antecedent, mentioned above, and of which an example is given in the first sentence in Exercise 15 below, allowance has to be made for the case of the relative being, as it is said, 'attracted', or conformed, to that of the antecedent, or *vice versa*.

Example:

ἐπὶ πᾶσιν οἷς ἤκουσαν (Luke 2. 20)
= over, *or* for, all things which they heard

The relative here, which should be gen. or acc. because governed by the verb ἀκούω, is conformed to the antecedent— dat., after ἐπί.

EXERCISE 15

A. Give English for:

οἶδα (= I know) [αὐτὸν, the true object of the verb, is suppressed] ᾧ πεπίστευκα. ἀκηκόαμεν αὐτοὶ τῆς αὐτοῦ φωνῆς. ἔστιν αὕτη ἡ ἀγγελία ἣν ἀκηκόαμεν ἀπ' αὐτοῦ. ἀγαπητοί, μὴ τῷ πνεύματι τούτῳ πιστεύετε. πολλοὶ ψευδοπροφῆται εἰς τὸν κόσμον εἰσι. ἡμεῖς μάρτυρές ἐσμεν τούτων. ἔσεσθέ μου μάρτυρες ἔν τε (= both) Ἰερουσαλὴμ καὶ ἐν τῇ Ἰουδαίᾳ.

B. Render into Greek:

The words of the witnesses whom we heard were just.   The disciple whom they heard is blind.   Ye yourselves heard his voice in the holy city.   Let them hear what (= that which, with suppression of the antecedent) he says to them.

SYNOPSIS OF TERMINATIONS—ACTIVE VOICE, THE INFINITIVE

136.

Present: ειν.

Future (cp. Present): σειν.

Aorist (without augment): σαι.

Perfect (with reduplication—see para. 115 (e)): κέναι.

The infinitive is not, strictly speaking, a 'mood', though often loosely referred to as such; it says nothing of the mood in which the subject of the sentence is, but is simply the abstract notion of the verb itself, distinguished as to kind of action as above—continuous, momentary, or completed, as in the moods already given.   It is a verbal noun, indeclinable in form, though its case when used as a noun will be shown by the def. art.

The sign of the inf. in English is 'to ...' (not to be confused with the preposition 'to', being etymologically distinct therefrom).   This 'to', however, does not invariably appear in

English, since, *e.g.*, 'I dare say' really means 'I dare to say'; this holds good after all such verbs as 'can'. A little reflection may be necessary before translating such a phrase from one language to another.

The English infinitive is often given as the meaning of the Greek form for the 1st pers. sing., pres. indic. act. Strictly speaking, this is incorrect; that is to say, *e.g.*, κελεύω does not mean 'to command' but 'I command'; the pres. inf. act. is, of course, κελεύειν, as shown above, and this is the form of the verb sometimes given. But the matter is not a serious one.

137. Rule 12. *The subject of a verb in the infinitive is put in the accusative case.* An example will be found in para. 138 (iv) (*a*). The construction has of course to be altered in the translation.

SOME USES OF THE INFINITIVE

138.

(i) *A verb in the infinitive may be the equivalent of a cognate noun.* This usage brings out the abstract notion of the verb.

Example:

τυφλοῖς πολλοῖς ἐχαρίσατο βλέπειν (Luke 7. 21)

= to many blind persons he freely gave sight

(ii) *An infinitive may depend on, and complete the idea of, an adjective.* This is in agreement with English construction.

Example:

οὗ οὐκ εἰμὶ ἱκανὸς λῦσαι τὸν ἱμάντα τῶν ὑποδημάτων αὐτοῦ (Luke 3. 16)

= the thong of whose sandals I am not competent to loosen (note the force of the aor. inf.—a single act)

(iii) *A verb in the infinitive may depend on another* (*finite*) *verb, completing the sense of the latter.* Some verbs do not of themselves give a complete sense, but need another verb to do this. 'He commands'—what? To do something; an action is commanded on the part of someone. Now while this may be expressed by ἵνα c. subj. ('command that someone do something'), as a matter of fact κελεύω is always followed in N.T. by the inf., thus agreeing with the English construction.

Examples:

οἱ στρατηγοὶ . . . ἐκέλευον ῥαβδίζειν (Acts 16. 22)
= the magistrates commanded to beat (them)
οὐδεὶς δύναται δυσὶ κυρίοις δουλεύειν (Mat. 6. 24)
= no one can serve two masters

(iv) *The infinitive may be used with a preposition to form a phrase.* The proper case called for by the preposition must of course be used for the def. art. The following are some N.T. examples of this common and interesting idiom.

(*a*) *Time.* The time during which, one action going on, another action takes place, is expressed by ἐν c. inf.

Example:

ἐν τῷ ἱερατεύειν αὐτὸν ἐν τῇ τάξει τῆς ἐφημερίας αὐτοῦ
(Luke 1. 8)
= while he served-as-priest in the appointed order of his class

This sentence illustrates Rule 12 above: the subject of the verb, in the English rendering ('he' = Zacharias), is in the acc. case in Greek, and the whole has to be recast accordingly.

(*b*) *Reason.* Διά c. acc. means 'because of', and is often used in this construction.

Example:

διὰ τὸ μὴ ἔχειν ῥίζαν (Mat. 13. 5)
= because it had no (because of the not to-have) root

(c) *Intention or purpose.* Either εἰς or πρός may be used.

Example:

εἰς τὸ θανατῶσαι αὐτόν (Mark 14. 55)
= with a view to putting him to death

This idea is often expressed by the use of the gen. case only.

Example:

τοῦ πιστεῦσαι αὐτῷ (Mat. 21. 32)
= so as to believe him

(v) *The infinitive may be the subject or the predicate of a sentence.* Sometimes the English participial form—really the gerund—is the equivalent of this: 'seeing is believing' = 'to see is to believe'. Here we have one inf. as the subject and another as the predicate. Or the predicate may be an adjective —'to err is human; to forgive, divine'.

Example:

αἰσχρόν ἐστι καὶ λέγειν (Eph. 5. 12)
= even to mention is disgraceful

139. The negative particle with the inf. may be either οὐ or μή. But since οὐ denies as a matter of fact, μή as a matter of thought, and since the inf. generally depends on a verb or clause involving thought, will, or design, the latter will generally be the appropriate negative.

Example:

λέγω ὑμῖν μὴ ὀμόσαι (Mat. 5. 34)
= I tell you not to swear

CLASSIFICATION OF TENSES

140. The tenses are divided by grammarians into two classes: (1) *Primary*—present, present-perfect, and future; and (2)

Historic—aorist, past-perfect, and imperfect. The latter are so called because they are concerned with past—that is to say, historic—action.

EXERCISE 16

A. Give English for:

ἐν τῷ σπείρειν αὐτόν. ἐν τῷ καθεύδειν τοὺς ἀνθρώπους. κεκέλευκε ὁ Θεὸς τοὺς ἀνθρώπους πιστεῦσαι τῷ εὐαγγελίῳ αὐτοῦ τῷ ἁγίῳ. λέγω ὑμῖν μὴ δακρύειν. καλόν ἐστι δουλεύειν Κυρίῳ. ὁ Ἰησοῦς μνημονεύειν τῶν ῥημάτων αὐτοῦ ἐκέλευσε τοὺς δώδεκα.

B. Render into Greek:

It is not good to worship the evil one. Christ did not command his disciples to fast.

C. Distinguish between—

ὁ Χριστὸς οὐκ ἐκέλευσε ἡμᾶς νηστεύειν. ὁ Χριστὸς ἡμᾶς ἐκέλευσε μὴ νηστεύειν.

SYNOPSIS OF TERMINATIONS—ACTIVE VOICE, THE PARTICIPLES

141.

Present:

| m., ων | f., ουσα | n., ον |

Future (cp. Present):

| σων | σουσα | σον |

Aorist (without augment):

| σας | σασα | σαν |

Perfect (with reduplication—see para. 115 (*e*)):

| κώς | κυῖα | κός |

As Professor A. T. Robertson remarks, Greek is 'a participle-loving language'; and in approaching the Greek participles we come to one of the most prominent features of the rich and

expressive verb system of that language.   In place of the only
two English forms—past and present respectively—'ed' or 't'
or 'ing', and but rarely used in the pl., we have the above
four tenses, each with different forms for the three genders,
and these declined for number and case.   Thus, as was
indicated in para. 15, participles fall under the two processes
of inflexion: their form as given above is arrived at in the course
of conjugating the verb, and they are then declined as adjectives.
This, indeed, accounts for their nomenclature—they participate
in the two parts of speech.   The participle is a verbal adjective,
as the infinitive (para. 136) is a verbal noun.

THE PARTICIPLE

(1) *Accidence*

142. As a verb, therefore, the participle has voice and tense;
as an adj. it has number, gender, and case.   Its accidence has
to do with the spelling of these its various forms, as follows:

Masculines in ων or σων (stem—οντ) are declined exactly like
λέων (para. 77), the aor. in σας (stem—σαντ) similarly (cp. πᾶς
in para. 98), and the perf. in κώς (stem—κοτ) as a dental (para.
79)—all, therefore, as 3rd-decl. nouns.

Feminines should cause no difficulty whatever, as all fem.
parts. without exception are declined exactly like fem. nouns of
the 1st decl.: those ending in σα like βασίλισσα (para. 18 (b)),
and the perf. act. like θύρα (para. 18 (c)).

Neuters.   Here the general rule must be borne in mind—
that neuters are alike in nom. and acc. in each number, and in
pl. end in short α (para. 17 (iii)).   Allowing for this, those
in ον, σον, σαν, and κός, are declined like their masc. counterparts in ων, σων, σας, and κώς, respectively, with the same
stems.

(2) *Syntax*

143. The syntax of the participle is concerned with its use in sentences, and this is, because of its dual character already spoken of, twofold: (*a*) as verb and (*b*) as adjective, which latter, with the def. art., is, in translating into English, equivalent to a noun (cp. para. 55).

144. (*a*) The Greek pres. or perf. part. can be used with εἶναι (paras. 39–41) as an auxiliary verb, as in English, to make a compound or periphrastic tense; this use is a step from the synthetic stage of a language to the analytic (para. 14), and is fairly frequent in Luke's writings.

Examples:

ἦν δὲ καὶ ὁ Ἰωάννης βαπτίζων ἐν Αἰνὼν ἐγγὺς τοῦ Σαλείμ, ὅτι ὕδατα πολλὰ ἦν ἐκεῖ (John 3. 23)
= now John also was baptizing in Ænon, near Salim, because there was much water there

καὶ ὡς ἀτενίζοντες ἦσαν εἰς τὸν οὐρανόν (Acts 1. 10)
= and as they were looking steadily into heaven

In such a construction, the part. must agree in number, gender, and case with the subject of the finite verb.

A perf. part. used with the pres. tense of εἰμι gives the proper present force of the pres.-perf. ind., while with imperf. a past-perf. meaning results.

145. A part. may be used to express action concurrently with or immediately preceding that of the finite verb, and/or in some way adding to the notion thereof.

Example:

ἐδίδασκεν αὐτοὺς λέγων (Mat. 5. 2)
= he taught them, saying

The use of the aor. part. in this way is one of the commonest idioms in the N.T., and must generally be represented in translation by two finite verbs—the action of the one (representing the part.) preceding or accompanying that of the other; or we may render by some such phrase as 'when . . .', 'after . . .', or 'having . . .'.

146. (*b*) It may be premised that it is not always easy to distinguish at first sight between the part. as verb and as adj.; the former, of course, denotes *action*, whereas the latter speaks of *state*, though one idea may easily shade off into the other.

147. As an adj., the Greek part. may be used like any other qualifying adj.—either with or without a noun. If used with a noun, the same principles apply in regard to its being predicative or attributive (para. 54).

Example:

Σὺ δὲ λάλει ἃ πρέπει τῇ ὑγιαινούσῃ διδασκαλίᾳ
(Tit. 2. 1; but cp. 1. 9, also ɪ Tim. 6. 3, etc.)
= but speak thou [doubly emphatic, by use and position] the things which become the health-giving teaching

148. But it is in its frequent use of the part. as an adj. with the def. art., but with the noun understood, that Greek best shows its participle-loving character. We have the usage in English, but to a limited extent only—*e.g.*, 'the missing', 'the takings', etc., expressions the meaning of which is obvious. Now Greek does this as a regular thing. In translating, a relative will commonly have to be used, or a noun substituted where no nearer equivalent exists, always noting, of course, the tense, gender, and number of the part. Thus, ὁ πιστεύων = the believing (man) = he who believes = the believer.

Examples:

Τάδε λέγει ὁ ἔχων τὰ ἑπτὰ πνεύματα τοῦ Θεοῦ καὶ τοὺς
ἑπτὰ ἀστέρας (Rev. 3. 1)
= these things says he who has the seven spirits of God
and the seven stars

μακαρία ἡ πιστεύσασα (Luke 1. 45)
= blessed is she who believed

The force of the aor. part. in the latter passage should be
noted: the reference is not to any continuous believing, but to
Mary's one act of faith at the Annunciation (1. 38).

149. The negatives are to be distinguished as hitherto—μή
when suppositions are made, οὐ when facts are stated; but the
distinction is occasionally somewhat difficult to see.

Examples:

οἱ μὴ πιστεύσαντες τῇ ἀληθείᾳ (II Thes. 2. 12)
= those who believe not the truth (*i.e.*, assuming the
existence of such persons)

ἡ οὐ τίκτουσα—ἡ οὐκ ὠδίνουσα (Gal. 4. 27)
= the not bearing—the not suffering birth-pangs [*i.e.*, a
woman is addressed as to whom such is actually the
position]

EXERCISE 17

Give English for:

οὐ χρείαν ἔχουσιν οἱ ἰσχύοντες ἰατροῦ ἀλλ' κακῶς οἱ ἔχοντες
[ἔχω κακῶς means 'I have (myself) ill = I am ill]. διὰ τί
ἡμεῖς καὶ οἱ Φαρισαῖοι νηστεύομεν, οἱ δὲ μαθηταί σου οὐ
νηστεύουσιν; ὁ τὸν λόγον μου ἀκούων ἔχει ζωὴν αἰώνιον. οἱ
μὴ πιστεύοντες τοῖς τοῦ Ἰησοῦ λόγοις τὴν ζωὴν τῶν αἰώνων
οὐκ ἔχουσιν. ὁ ἔχων οὖς ἀκουσάτω τι τὸ πνεῦμα λέγει ταῖς
ἐκκλησίαις.

UNCONTRACTED VERBS—A 1

150. All the verbs with which we have so far been concerned
have their stems ending in a close vowel (ι or υ) or a diphthong
incorporating one of them; and in such verbs, it may once
more be said, the stem remains unaltered throughout all voices,
moods, tenses, numbers, and persons, their conjugation being
simply a matter of adding the appropriate termination, from
the synopses given, to the stem, with augment and/or reduplication when called for. The very rare exceptions to this are
easily remembered, and are explained by their history: κλαίω
(I wail), *e.g.*, which has κλαύσω for its fut. ind. act., does so
because its stem really ends in the old letter *digamma* (κλαϝ),
which thus reappears as υ (cp., for nouns, para. 82).

These verbs, in the classification shown here, are thus called
A 1 verbs, and they are the simplest of all.

CLASSIFICATION OF VERBS OF THE FIRST CONJUGATION
Vowel Stems

A 1—Close-vowel stems (ι, υ; αι, ει; αυ, ευ, ου). Uncontracted; the terminations are simply added to the unaltered stem. The only exceptions are the insertion of σ
before dental terminations in ἀκούω, etc., and αι may
become αυ in fut.

A 2—Open-vowel stems (α, ε, or ο). Contracted: the final
vowel of the stem coalesces with the initial vowel of the
termination in pres. and imperf. (see para. 151 (*b*)).

Consonant Stems

B 3—Short monosyllabic stems (in the main), ending in a
guttural or a labial (λέγ-ω, βλέπ-ω), but not a liquid.

B 4—Stems ending in ζ, when not a softening of a guttural
(καθαρίζ-ω).

B 5*—Stems modified by the lengthening of the radical vowel
(λείπ-ω; stem, λιπ).

* These verbs may have second aorist and other alternative tenses.

B 6*—Stems modified by the insertion of τ (τύπτ-ω; stem, τυπ).

B 7*—Stems modified by the insertion of the syllable αν, with or without further modification (μανθάν-ω; stem μαθ).

B 8*—Stems ending in σκ. This element, with preceding vowel, is a modifying insertion (εὑρίσκ-ω; stem, εὑρ).

B 9*—Stems ending in σσ or ττ—the softening of a guttural (τάσσ-ω; stem, ταγ).

B 10*—Liquid stems (κρίν-ω).

CONTRACTED VERBS—A 2

151. Attention must now be directed to a triple class of open-vowel (α, ε, or ο) stems, classified as A 2. No verbal stem can end in η or ω, so that these two classes exhaust the possibilities of vowel stems.

Now an examination of the six synopses given will reveal that in the pres. tenses throughout, and in the imperf. ind., the terminations begin with a vowel, whereas in all the other tenses they begin with a consonant. One of two things, therefore, has to be done.

(a) If the termination begins with a consonant, it is still a matter of adding it to the stem, but the α or ε of the stem is generally—not invariably—lengthened to η, and ο is always lengthened to ω. An example of each will make this clear.

ἀγαπάω (= I love); fut. ind., ἀγαπήσω; aor., ἠγάπησα (temporal augment—para. 131); pres.-perf., ἠγάπηκα (improper reduplication—para. 132); aor. part., ἀγαπήσας; and so on, the conjugation being perfectly regular and consistent once the lengthening of the stem vowel is allowed for. On the other hand, some verbs (e.g., γελάω, I laugh) do not lengthen the α at all. Whether a particular α or ε verb does or does not must be learnt from a lexicon.

* These verbs may have second aorist and other alternative tenses.

φωνέω (I utter a sound): fut. ind., φωνήσω; aor. inf., φωνῆσαι,
    etc. But again, καλέω (I call), e.g., does not lengthen the
    ε—though, as will be seen later, a different sort of change
    occurs in some tenses.

σταυρόω (I crucify): aor. ind., ἐσταύρωσα. Verbs the stem of
    which ends in o invariably lengthen this to ω.

(b) If the termination begins with a vowel, then, obviously,
two vowels come together, and this involves contraction; hence
the term by which they are known. This contraction takes
place quite regularly, in accordance with the table here given.
Eight vowel sounds are involved as to terminations, these being
the only ones with which such can begin; and, of course, three
as to stems. On the one hand, then, by the use of this table
any verb of this class can be conjugated in the two tenses (pres.
and imperf.) concerned; and, on the other, any given verb
form analysed and placed.

TABLE OF VOWEL CONTRACTIONS

Stem ending	First letter of termination							
	ω	ει	ο	ε	ου	η	ῃ	οι
α	ω	ᾳ*	ω	α	ω	α	ᾳ	ῳ
ε	ω	ει	ου	ει	ου	η	ῃ	οι
ο	ω	οι†	ου	ου	ου	ω	οι	οι

* Sometimes only α in infinitives in ειν.

† ου in infinitives in ειν.

Two features in this table should be noted, as a help to its
acquisition; one is that an o sound always predominates in the
resultant long vowel or diphthong; and the other is that an ι

is never lost, but reappears as subscript or in a diphthong, except as in the footnote.

Examples of Use. It is desired to know what ἐλαλοῦμεν means. It has the augment, and therefore belongs to the ind. mood, and so is an imperf. tense form; the table shows that ου results from ε or ο followed by ο or ου; the syllable μεν restricts us to ο (ομεν); a verb λαλέω (I speak) will be found in the lexicon; ἐλαλοῦμεν is, therefore really ἐλαλέ-ομεν = we were speaking.

Again, what is the 3rd pers. pl. pres. imp. act. of τιμάω (I honour)? The termination is έτωσαν (para. 122); therefore the form is τιμα-έτωσαν, which by the table becomes τιμάτωσαν = let them honour.

It is the *un*contracted form of the 1st pers. sing. pres. ind. of these verbs which is given in lexicons, and in dealing with them grammatically as above; but in continuous texts, the proper contracted form (ἀγαπῶ, φωνῶ, σταυρῶ) is used.

Note on Accentuation. If the former of the two vowels has the acute, the resulting long vowel or diphthong carries the circumflex; if the latter, the acute remains. The examples given show this, and para. 11 throws further light on the matter.

Allowance being made for these contractions in this A 2 class of verbs, the learner should now once for all grasp the fact that *all Greek verbs are, without exception, absolutely regular in all their present tenses, and that the imperfect (ind.) regularly follows the present as to stem.* The study of the verb is thus advanced a definite stage, and only consonant stems in the other tenses remain to be considered, with the terminations for the middle and passive voices throughout.

VOCABULARY

152. A few commonly used adjective-pronouns may be noted—all declined regularly as adjectives of the first form (para. 51):

ἄλλος, η, ο (see para. 67)

ἕτερος, α, ον, another (of a different kind) (see para. 67)

ἕκαστος, η, ον, each

ἀλλήλων (plur. only), one another

EXERCISE 18

Give English for:

φιλεῖς με; ὑμεῖς ἐστε τὸ ἅλας τῆς γῆς καὶ τὸ φῶς τοῦ κόσμου. ὁ ἐμὲ μισῶν καὶ τὸν πατέρα μου μισεῖ. μακάριοι οἱ πεινῶντες καὶ διψῶντες τὴν δικαιοσύνην. ὁ κόσμος ἐμὲ μεμίσηκεν. ὅτι ταῦτα λελάληκα ὑμῖν ἡ λύπη πεπλήρωκεν ὑμῶν τὴν καρδίαν. τετήρηκαν τὸν λόγον σου. ἀγαπῶμεν ἀλλήλους. Πάτερ ἅγιε, τήρησον αὐτοὺς ἐν τῷ ὀνόματί σου. σὺ εἶ Πέτρος, καὶ ἐπὶ ταύτῃ τῇ πέτρᾳ οἰκοδομήσω μου τὴν ἐκκλησίαν, καὶ πύλαι ᾅδου οὐ κατισχύσουσιν αὐτῆς. Διδάσκαλε ἀγαθέ, τί ποιήσας ζωὴν αἰώνιον κληρονομήσω; ἀγαπήσεις Κύριον τὸν Θεόν σου.

THE GENITIVE ABSOLUTE

153. This peculiarly Greek construction, to which reference was made in para. 22 (iii), can now be taken. It consists of a noun or pronoun and a participle, agreeing as to number and gender, and both in the genitive case, but not grammatically related to the principal sentence; that is to say, the phrase stands by itself as an independent conception.

In English we have the nominative absolute: 'I being in the way, the Lord led me'—where 'I' and 'being' are respectively pronoun and participle in apposition with each other, but independent grammatically of the sentence, with its finite verb, following, though of course adding to it in thought. In Latin the analogous construction is the ablative absolute, of which the familiar *Deo volente* (God willing) is an example. In Greek the construction is used to indicate some accessory of time, manner, or circumstance; and a suitable conjunction must be supplied in translating, with the altered construction.

Example :

ἀναχωρησάντων δὲ αὐτῶν (Mat. 2. 13)
= now when they departed

THE VERB 'TO BE'
Concluded (see paras. 39–41)

154. *Present Imperative:*

ἴσθι, be thou	ἔστε, be ye
ἔστω *or* ἤτω, let him be	ἔστωσαν, let them be

155. *Present Subjunctive:*

ὦ, I may be	ὦμεν, we may be
ᾖς, thou	ἦτε, ye
ᾖ, he, she, *or* it	ὦσι(ν), they

156. *Present Optative:*

εἴην, I might be	εἴημεν, we might be
εἴης, thou	εἴητε, ye
εἴη, he, she, *or* it	εἴησαν, they

157. *The Infinitive:*
Pres.—εἶναι, to be
Fut.—ἔσεσθαι, to be about to be

158. *The Participles:*
Pres.—ὤν, οὖσα, ὄν, being
Fut.—ἐσόμενος, -η, -ον, about to be

159. The general features of all verb forms can be recognized here—a long vowel being characteristic of the subj. mood, and a diphthong of the opt. Several tenses are wanting, and the student now has all there are in this particular verb.

The pres. part. masc. is of interest, because it was used by the Seventy, in Exod. 3. 14 and elsewhere, as the Greek equivalent of the Hebrew name rendered 'I AM' in English, and reappears with this connotation in N.T., at Rev. 1. 4: ὁ ὤν (*lit.* the Being) = the One who is.

The various tenses may all be used, as in English, to make up, with participles, analytic forms of other verbs—that is, εἰμί is used as an auxiliary verb. In some instances, as will be seen later, this is the only possible form.

THE MIDDLE AND PASSIVE VOICES

160. The student is now in possession of all the terminations of the active voice of Greek verbs in ω, or of the 1st conj. (paras. 116, 122, 124, 130, 136, and 141)—that is, of the overwhelming majority of Greek verbs (all but about three dozen so far as N.T. is concerned).

As regards accidence, the ground must now be gone over again for the middle and passive voices (para. 112), taken together for this purpose. The terminations for these voices should be compared with those for the active voice in the same tense, as points of similarity will be observed and the memory thereby assisted.

It will be seen from the scheme of terminations below (para. 162) that only in the aorist and future tenses are there separate forms for the two voices—the mid. first, and the pass. below it; in all the other tenses one form does duty for both, and their differentiation is a matter of interpretation. This holds good throughout the verb.

As to syntax, side by side with likenesses there are differences due to the different action involved. We will consider the passive voice first.

161. Roughly stated, the passive voice connotes action in the reverse direction to that of the active; the subject of the verb suffers an action instead of performing one. Action there is, of course, in both instances; but the terms 'active' and 'passive' are used from the standpoint of the subject, which must still be in the nominative case. This creates the grammatical paradox—that the *subject* of a passive verb is really the *object* of the action indicated. For example—

$$\text{ἄγω} = \text{I lead; ἄγομαι} = \text{I am led}$$

In the first form, the pronoun subject of the verb ('I') performs an action—that of leading; such a verb might be used intransitively, but if used transitively it would of course have a direct object in the accusative case—that on which the action is performed. In the second of the above verb forms, however, while the action is the same, it is in the opposite direction; instead of proceeding outward from him to an object, it proceeds inward to him as its object; he suffers the action instead of performing it; he is passive, not active.

Now this difference of action is normally expressed in Greek, not by the analytic method, as in English, of employing auxiliary verbs with the participle of the verb being conjugated, but by the synthetic method of changing the termination while retaining the same verbal stem (para. 14). The exceptions are the few forms where the demands of euphony make synthesis impossible, and then recourse is had to analysis (see para. 159).

Uncontracted vowel stems (A 1—para. 150) can still be conjugated unchanged, as for the active forms. A few of these, however, as well as some ε verbs, insert σ before a dental (ἠκούσθη = it was heard; τετέλεσται = it has been, *i.e.* is, finished, as in John 19. 30). Further, in accordance with a rule in Greek that consecutive syllables must not begin each with an aspirate (though there are exceptions to this), such a stem as θυ becomes τυ if an aspirate follows (ἐτύθη = he was slain, as in 1 Cor. 5. 8).

Contracted vowel stems (A 2—para. 151) are dealt with according to the table given.

SYNOPSIS OF TERMINATIONS—MIDDLE AND PASSIVE VOICES, INDICATIVE MOOD

162.

Present:

ομαι	η	εται	όμεθα	εσθε	ονται

Imperfect (with augment—see para. 115 (*d*)):

όμην	ου	ετο	όμεθα	εσθε	οντο

Aorist (with augment):

σάμην	σω	σατο	σάμεθα	σασθε	σαντο
θην	θης	θη	θημεν	θητε	θησαν

Future (cp. Present):

σομαι	ση	σεται	σόμεθα	σεσθε	σονται
θήσομαι	θήσῃ	θήσεται	θησόμεθα	θήσεσθε	θήσονται

Pres.-Perfect (with reduplication—see para. 115 (*e*)):

μαι	σαι	ται	μεθα	σθε	νται

Past-Perfect (with augment and reduplication—see para. 115 (*f*)):

μην	σο	το	μεθα	σθε	ντο

The fut. mid., like the fut. act., is formed from the pres. by inserting σ between stem and termination; then the pass. is formed from the mid. by the further insertion of the element θη. The connection between the pres. and imperf. and the pres.-perf. and past-perf. respectively should be noted: the terminations are the same, except that in the perf. tenses there is no connecting vowel (η is really εσαι, and ου is εσο, with the σ dropped in both instances, resulting in vowel contraction).

163. Rule 13. *Agency after a passive verb is expressed by ὑπό with the genitive case.*

Example:

ὁ ἀγαπῶν με ἀγαπηθήσεται ὑπὸ τοῦ πατρός μου
(John 14. 21)
= he who loves me shall be loved by my Father

Precisely the same action would be described by an active verb thus—

ὁ πατήρ μου ἀγαπήσει αὐτόν (John 14. 23)
= my Father will love him

EXERCISE 19

A. Give English for:

πάντες οἱ πιστεύοντες εἰς τὸ τοῦ Ἰησοῦ Χριστοῦ ὄνομα ἐν τῇ βασιλείᾳ αὐτοῦ εἰσι. ἡ ἐκκλησία μου ἐπὶ (on) ταύτῃ τῇ πέτρᾳ οἰκοδομηθήσεται. πάντα μοί ἐστι. οὗτος ὁ ἀνὴρ τὴν συναγωγὴν ἡμῶν ᾠκοδόμησε. ἄκοντα τὰ παιδία. πᾶς ὁ μου τῆς φωνῆς ἀκούων ἄκουε καὶ τοῦ πατρός. οἱ τοῦ θεοῦ υἱοὶ ἄγονται ὑπὸ τοῦ πνεύματος αὐτοῦ. αἱ ἐντολαὶ αὐτοῦ βαρεῖαι οὐκ εἰσιν. ἠγόμην ἐγὼ ὑπὸ τοῦ Ἰησοῦ πνεύματος. τὸ εὐαγγέλιον ἡμῶν ἐπιστεύθη.

B. Give the passive forms corresponding to the following active:

ἤγομεν, φιλήσετε, πιστεύει, ἄγεις.

SYNOPSIS OF TERMINATIONS—MIDDLE AND PASSIVE VOICES, IMPERATIVE MOOD

164.

Present:

—	ου	ἔσθω	—	εσθε	ἔσθωσαν

Aorist (without augment):

—	σαι	σάσθω	—	σασθε	σάσθωσαν
—	θητι	θήτω	—	θητε	θήτωσαν

Perfect (with reduplication—see para. 115 (*e*)):

—	σο	σθω	—	σθε	σθωσαν

165. The middle voice may now be considered. This, as its name implies, occupies a position midway between the other two voices. Its use and force will become apparent as progress is made in other respects; but, briefly, it suggests that the action of the particular verb in question begins and ends with the subject (cp. the reflexive verbs in French: *s'élever* = to get up, as distinguished from *élever* = to lift, raise, *or* bring up). If τύπτω means 'I strike', then τύπτομαι, if passive, means 'I am struck', but if middle 'I strike myself'. The context would give the necessary guidance, and the usage of each verb must be considered in translating.

The force of the middle voice is sometimes expressed by the active voice with the appropriate reflexive pronoun.

Example:

ἐγὼ ἁγιάζω ἐμαυτόν (John 17. 19)
= I sanctify myself

Some active verbs of frequent occurrence have a fut. and/or aor. in the mid. form, instead of or as well as the act., but without change of meaning: αἰτέω = I ask, αἰτήσομαι = I shall ask.

COMPOUND VERBS

166. As in English, so in Greek—a simple verb may have a preposition prefixed to it, more or less modifying its meaning, and producing a compound verb. From 'take' we form '*under*take', '*over*take', and so on.

There are in Greek eighteen prepositions, called 'proper', governing different cases of nouns when used as such; some of these have been given, but for clearness' sake a complete list is given in para. 168.   These eighteen only are used in composition with verbs, and one of them being not so used in N.T. leaves seventeen for consideration in this respect.   On the other hand, the simple verb may not occur at all, or not in N.T., but only in some one or more compounded forms.

It is quite common for a preposition to be used as part of a compound verb, and then to be repeated before a governed noun, though this does not always happen.   But the learner must not hastily assume that a compound verb will of itself govern the same case as the preposition concerned, for this by no means follows; and that it could not will readily be seen from the fact that a verb may be compounded with two prepositions which by themselves govern two different cases— thus: σύν (= with) takes the dat., ἀπό (= from) the gen., but the compound verb συναποστέλλω (I send forth together) has the acc.

Euphonic changes must be allowed for in these verbs: ἐκ becomes ἐξ before a vowel, as stated in para. 48 (ἐκ + ἄγω becomes ἐξάγω = I lead out); ἐν and σύν become— though editions of N.T. vary in this—ἐγ and συγ before gutturals (ἐν + κρύπτω, ἐγκρύπτω = I hide within), and the latter συλ before λ and μ before a labial or μ.

If a simple verb beginning with a vowel is compounded with a preposition ending in one, this last is dropped (ἀνά + ἀγγέλλω becomes ἀναγγέλλω = I announce or report).   It must be remembered, however, that περί and πρό never elide their final letters.

The prefixed preposition may simply add to the idea of the simple verb in an obvious way, as in the examples just given— out, in, again; or it may intensify or otherwise modify it: γινώσκω = I know, ἐπιγινώσκω = I know fully, while ἀναγινώσκω has the meaning 'I read (aloud)'—perhaps from the idea of recognizing the written characters.

Augment and Reduplication in Compound Verbs

167. The augment or reduplication is inserted between the preposition and the simple verb, not placed before the verb as a whole; and the rules of vowel elision and euphonic change then come into operation. A few examples will make this clear: from λέγω (= I say) is formed ἐκλέγομαι (I choose), of which the aor. ind. mid. is ἐξελεξάμην, γ and σ giving ξ, and the perf. ind. pass. ἐκλέλεγμαι; of ἀναγγέλλω the imperf. act. is ἀνήγγελλον.

In some compound verbs the preposition has become so closely attached to the simple stem as not to be separable from it, or the apparently simple verb may not really exist as such; in either of these events the augment or reduplication will precede, as ἐπροφήτευσα, though the erroneous form προεφήτευσα does occur.

VOCABULARY

168. The seventeen proper prepositions referred to in para. 166 are as follows. Much thought and care is necessary in dealing with them, but they well repay the closest study. We can give here only the most obvious meanings of some of them.

Gen. only: ἀντί, against, instead of; ἀπό, away from, from (the outside); ἐκ, ἐξ, out, out of, from (the inside); πρό, before, in front of.

Dat. only: ἐν, in, (with plurals) among, by; σύν with.

Acc. only: ἀνά, up, again; εἰς, in (thus sometimes indistinguishable from ἐν, though the latter never means 'into'), into, to, toward, unto.

Gen. or *Acc.*: διά, G. through, by means of, A. on account of, because of; κατά, G. against, A. according to, throughout, during, over; μετά, G. with, A. after; περί, G. concerning, A. round about; ὑπέρ, G. on behalf of, A. above; ὑπό, G. by, A. under.

Gen., Dat., or *Acc.*: ἐπί, G. on, over, D. upon, on account of, A. unto; παρά, G. from, D. near, A. beside, beyond, contrary to; πρός, G. for, D. at, close by, A. toward, with.

The remaining proper preposition, occurring in N.T. only in composition with verbs, is ἀμφί, which when so used means 'about, around, *or* doubly'.

EXERCISE 20

Give English for:

φιμώθητι. πεφίμωσο. πολὺ πλανᾶσθε. συ εἶ ὁ υἱὸς τοῦ Θεοῦ τοῦ ζῶντος. ἅγιοι τῷ Χριστῷ συμβασιλεύσουσιν. οὐκ ἔστιν Θεὸς νεκρῶν ἀλλὰ ζώντων. ἑαυτοὺς πλανῶμεν. μετὰ ταῦτα ἄνθρωπος πλούσιος ἀπὸ Ἀριμαθαίας, τοὔνομα Ἰωσήφ, ὃς καὶ αὐτὸς ἐμαθητεύθη τῷ Ἰησοῦ, ᾐτήσατο τὸ σῶμα τοῦ Ἰησοῦ. ὁ Παῦλος διώδευσε τὴν Ἀμφίπολιν. ὁ ἄνεμος καὶ ἡ θάλασσα ὑπήκουον αὐτόν. ἄγγελος ἀπ' οὐρανοῦ ἐνίσχυσεν τὸν Ἰησοῦν.

SYNOPSIS OF TERMINATIONS—MIDDLE AND PASSIVE VOICES, SUBJUNCTIVE MOOD

169.

Present:

ωμαι	η	ηται	ώμεθα	ησθε	ωνται

Aorist (without augment):

σωμαι	ση	σηται	σώμεθα	σησθε	σωνται
θῶ	θῇς	θῇ	θῶμεν	θῆτε	θῶσι

Perfect:

Made by the perf. pass. part. (para. 184), with εἰμί as an auxiliary verb.

170. Rule 14. *The subjunctive mood (including the optative) cannot, strictly speaking, stand in an independent sentence.* If it appears to do so, it is because of some unexpressed idea, or the construction is to be otherwise explained.

Example:

μὴ φοβηθῇς (Mat. 1. 20)
= fear thou not

Here the aor. pass. of φοβέομαι (I am fearful) is used imperatively; see paras. 112, 117.

CONSONANT STEMS
General Remarks

171. Having disposed, in paras. 150 and 151, of all the verbs the stems of which end in a vowel, we may now take in order the consonant stems—the eight B verbs, 3–10, in our classification. In all these, without exception, once the stem is recognized conjugation may proceed with perfect regularity in all the present tenses; moreover, as the imperfect always follows the present, this also can be conjugated without fear of going astray. For instance—

Ind.—τύπτ-ω, I strike
Imperat.—τύπτ-ε, strike thou
Subj.—τύπτ-ω, I may strike
Opt.—τύπτ-οιμι, I might strike
Part.—τύπτ-ων, striking
Inf.—τύπτ-ειν, to strike
Imperf.—ἔτυπτ-ον, I was striking

Beyond this the learner cannot at this stage go, as, for one thing, a particular verb may be defective as to some or all of the remaining tenses, and, for another, in all those other tenses the terminations begin with a consonant; this means, in the case of consonant stems, that two consonants come together, and so questions of euphony arise.

DEPONENT VERBS

172. A modification must be introduced into the conception of the middle and passive voices as set forth in paras. 160 and 161. This is that some verbs have no active form, but only a passive, and/or a middle, though with an active meaning. Such verbs are known as 'deponents'. No fresh terminations have to be learnt—it is simply a matter of the use of the mid. or pass. terminations instead of the act. No absolute rule can be laid down, as some verbs oscillate between the two voices. Thus—

πορεύ-ομαι, I go, travel, journey
πορεύσομαι, I shall go
ἐπορεύθην, I went

173. Rule 15. *Two or more nouns (including participles) 'in apposition'—that is to say, referring to the same person or thing—are put in the same case.*

Example:

ἐν ἡμέραις Ἡρώδου τοῦ βασιλέως (Mat. 2. 1)
= in the days of Herod the king

Here the nouns 'Herod' and 'king' refer to the same person, and are therefore in the same case.

VOCABULARY

174. καλέω (= I call, invite) undergoes a change in the passive voice—the stem καλε becomes κλη (cp. κλῆσις = a calling): aor. ind. ἐκλήθην, fut. ind. κληθήσομαι, and so of the other tenses.

EXERCISE 21

Give English for:

Ναζαραῖος κληθήσεται. υἱοὶ Θεοῦ κληθήσονται. μὴ κληθῆτε ῥαββί, μηδὲ κληθῆτε καθηγηταί. σύ, παιδίον, προφήτης Ὑψίστου κληθήσῃ. πορεύου εἰς τὸν οἶκόν σου, ὁ υἱός σου ζῇ. πορεύσομαι πρὸς τὸν πατέρα μου. ὁ διδάσκων ἕτερον σεαυτὸν οὐ διδάσκεις; ἐφοβοῦντο τὸν λαόν. οὐδεὶς τῶν ἀνδρῶν ἐκείνων γεύσεταί μου τοῦ δείπνου. μὴ φοβηθῆτε αὐτούς. διδάσκων ἦν ὁ Ἰησοῦς ἐν μιᾷ τῶν συναγωγῶν αὐτῶν. τὸ αἷμα Ἰησοῦ Χριστοῦ υἱοῦ Θεοῦ καθαρίζει ἡμᾶς ἀπὸ πάσης ἁμαρτίας. ὁ ἀκούων τοὺς λόγους μου καὶ πιστεύων εἰς ἐμὲ οὐ μὴ γεύσηται θανάτου.

SYNOPSIS OF TERMINATIONS—MIDDLE AND PASSIVE VOICES, OPTATIVE MOOD

175.

Present:

| οίμην | οιο | οιτο | οίμεθα | οισθε | οιντο |

Aorist (without augment):

| σαίμην | σαιο | σαιτο | σαίμεθα | σαισθε | σαιντο |
| θείην | θείης | θείη | θείημεν | θείητε | θείησαν |

It should be noticed again how diphthongal sounds characterize these endings, as in the active voice. The above two tenses, it may also be repeated, are all that occur in N.T.; even these are rare, but are given here for completeness' sake (para. 130).

VERBS: CONSONANT STEMS

Class B 3

176. The simplest form of consonant stem is that which consists of a short monosyllable, ending in a single consonant other than a liquid, incapable of simplification, and recognizable at once throughout its conjugation when the requirements of orthography and euphony are allowed for. In such a verb, the stem is also a root from which a cognate noun is—or may be—formed, and so the verb is a 'root-verb'. An example is ἄρχω in mid. (ἄρχομαι) = I begin, the stem of which is seen in ἀρχή (beginning) and in derivatives. The student will find it both interesting and helpful as an aid to memory thus to link up verbs and nouns, etc.

Some polysyllabic stems have to be included in this B 3 class, and others that do not strictly conform to the above description; guidance will be given as to this in course.

A glance at the synopses of terminations being given will show that the terminations of the only tenses with which we are now concerned (fut., aor., and the two perfs.) begin with one or other of six consonants—μ, σ (including σθ), τ, κ, θ, and ν; the last, occurring (in the combination ντ) in the 3rd pers. pl. of the perfs. pass., cannot be accommodated anyhow to a preceding consonant, so the 'periphrastic perfect passive' is used—the pass. part. with εἰμί as an auxiliary verb (cp. para. 169). This leaves five varieties of combination, and the principles on which this is done are now to be given, restricting ourselves for the present to labial or guttural stems, which together pretty well make up class B 3.

Consonant Combinations

177. When μ follows, a labial must be changed into μ, a sharp or aspirated guttural into the flat γ. Thus, from τρίβω (I rub), pres.-perf. ind. pass. τέτριμμαι for τε-τριβ-μαι (I have been rubbed); from διδάσκω (see vocabulary below) (I teach), δεδίδαγμαι for δε-διδακ-μαι (I have been taught).

When σ follows, any labial becomes ψ, and any guttural becomes ξ. Thus—from γράφω (I write), aor. ind. act. ἔγραψα for ἐ-γραφ-σα (I wrote); from λέγω (I say), aor. inf. act. λέξαι for λεγ-σαι (to say). With σθ, the σ is dropped altogether, and the resulting combination dealt with according to the rules for a following θ as below. Thus—from τρίβω, pres.-perf. ind. pass. τέτριφθε for τε-τριβ-σθε (ye have been rubbed).

When τ follows, a flat or aspirated labial or guttural must be sharpened to π or κ respectively. Thus—from θλίβω (I press), pres.-perf. ind. pass. τέθλιπται for τε-θλιβ-ται (he has been pressed); from ἄγω (I lead), same tense ἦκται for ἦγ-ται (he has been led).

When κ follows, a flat or sharp labial or guttural is aspirated and the κ dropped, and after an aspirated labial or guttural the κ is dropped without further change. Thus—from τρίβω, pres.-perf. ind. act. τέτριφα for τε-τριβ-κα (I have rubbed); from ἄγω, same tense ἦχα for ἦγ-κα (I have led); from γράφω, γέγραφα for γε-γραφ-κα (I have written).

When θ follows, a flat or sharp labial or guttural must be changed into its corresponding aspirate. Thus—from πέμπω (I send), aor. ind. pass. ἐπέμφθη for ἐ-πεμπ-θη (he was sent); from ἄγω, same tense ἤχθη for ἦγ-θη (he was led).

The above rules are of general application, and are based on the principles laid down in para. 10.

178. Rule 16. γάρ (for) *and* δέ (and, but, now) *are said to be post-positive*—that is, they cannot stand first in a sentence, though of course are taken first in translating into English.

VOCABULARY

179. A point to note in some verbs is the shifting of the aspirate. ἔχω (I have) makes ἕξω for fut. ind.—that is, the aspirate, being lost from χ in conjugation, is preserved over initial ε. In τρέφω (I feed; ἀνατρέφω, nourish, bring up) the aspirate passes from φ to τ—aor. ind. ἔθρεψα.

διώκω (I chase, follow, pursue, persecute), though of two syllables as to its stem, belongs to this B 3 class.

διδάσκω (I teach) is, like all Greek verbs, regularly conjugated in its pres. and imperf. tenses, but all other tenses are from a stem διδακ. The pres. stem is seen in the noun διδάσκαλος (teacher) and the latter in the adjective διδακτός (taught).

EXERCISE 22

Give English for:

βλέψον εἰς ἡμᾶς. ὃ βλέπεις γράψον εἰς βιβλίον καὶ πέμψον ταῖς ἑπτὰ ἐκκλησίαις. ἔγραψεν Μωϋσῆς περὶ Ἰησοῦ. ὃ γέγραφα, γέγραφα. περὶ δὲ ὧν ἐγράψατέ μοι. οὕτως ἐδίωξαν τοὺς προφήτας τοὺς πρὸ ὑμῶν. τί με διώκεις; διωχθήσεσθε ἀπὸ πόλεως εἰς πόλιν. ὑμᾶς διδάξει πάντα. ὁ Θεὸς τῆς εἰρήνης συντρίψει τὸν σατανᾶν ὑπὸ τοὺς πόδας ὑμῶν ἐν τάχει. ἐθρέψαμέν σε. ἡ θυγάτηρ Φαραὼ ἀνεθρέψατο Μωϋσῆν ἑαυτῇ εἰς υἱόν. στρέψον αὐτῷ καὶ τὴν ἄλλην σιαγόνα. ἐρωτῶ σε οὖν, πάτερ, ἵνα πέμψῃς Λάζαρον εἰς τὸν οἶκον τοῦ πατρός μου· ἔχω γὰρ πέντε ἀδελφούς.

SYNOPSIS OF TERMINATIONS—MIDDLE AND PASSIVE VOICES, THE INFINITIVE

180.

Present: εσθαι

Future (cp. present): σεσθαι

θήσεσθαι

Aorist (without augment): σασθαι

θῆναι

Perfect (with reduplication—see para. 115 (e)): σθαι

VERBS: CONSONANT STEMS

Class B 4

181. There are quite a number of verbs the stem of which ends in ζ, and these may be taken together as constituting a simple and easily managed class. Some verbs, indeed, whose lexical form is -ζω or -ζομαι have guttural stems, and the ζ is in these a softening of the hard guttural, somewhat after the fashion of the softening of the *t* in English in the termination -*tion*. Such a verb is κράζω (= I cry out); the true stem of this is κραγ. The fut. ind. decides the classification of these verbs, that tense of κράζω being κράξω, not κράσω, as it would be if it were a B 4 verb. Allowing for this anomaly, κράζω is a regular B 3 verb.

The verbs with which we are now concerned have dental stems, the phonetic value of ζ being *dz* (para. 2). With them may be taken verbs in the simple dentals δ, τ, and θ, to which the same rules apply as are now given for the ζ verbs.

Consonant Combinations

182. Followed by μ, ζ becomes σ (note the rule for pronunciation in para. 8). Thus—from ἁγιάζω (I sanctify), pres.-perf. ind. pass. ἡγίασμαι (I have been sanctified).

Followed by σ, ζ disappears altogether. Thus—from δοξάζω (I glorify), aor. ind. act. ἐδόξασαν (they glorified).

Followed by τ, ζ becomes σ. Thus—from δοκιμάζω (I approve), pres.-perf. ind. pass. δεδοκίμασται (he has been approved).

Followed by κ, ζ either becomes σ or is dropped entirely. Thus—from ἐλπίζω (I hope), pres.-perf. ind. act. ἠλπίκαμεν (we have hoped).

Followed by θ, ζ becomes σ or may be dropped. Thus—from ἀγοράζω (I buy), aor. ind. pass. ἠγοράσθη (it was bought); from σώζω (I heal *or* save) aor. inf. pass. σωθῆναι (to be healed).

VOCABULARY

183. ἐλπίζω = I hope, and a few other B 4 verbs, have what is known as the 'Attic future'—a contracted form (ἐλπιῶ, etc.), as though it were formed from an ε stem, with contraction according to the table in para. 151, the ζ being dropped entirely.

EXERCISE 23

Give English for:

τὸ πνεῦμα τῆς ἀληθείας ἐμὲ δοξάσει. ἐδόξασε τὸν Θεὸν
Ἰσραήλ. δόξασόν σου τὸ ὄνομα. δεδόξασμαι ἐν αὐτοῖς.
κύριε, σῶσον ἡμᾶς. καλέσεις τὸ ὄνομα αὐτοῦ Ἰησοῦν, αὐτὸς
γὰρ σώσει τὸν λαὸν αὐτοῦ ἀπὸ τῶν ἁμαρτιῶν αὐτῶν. ἡ
πίστις σου σέσωκέ σε. ἐσώθη ἡ γυνή. ταῦτα λέγω, ἵνα ὑμεῖς
σωθῆτε. ἄλλους ἔσωσε, σωσάτω ἑαυτόν. ζεύγη βοῶν ἠγόρασα
πέντε. τούτους ἀποστόλους ὠνόμασε. ἡγίασται ὁ ἀνὴρ ὁ
ἄπιστος ἐν τῇ γυναικί, καὶ ἡγίασται ἡ γυνὴ ἡ ἄπιστος ἐν τῷ
ἀδελφῷ.

SYNOPSIS OF TERMINATIONS—MIDDLE AND PASSIVE VOICES, PARTICIPLES

184.

Present:

| m. όμενος | f. ομένη | n. όμενον |

Future (cp. Present):

| σόμενος | σομένη | σόμενον |
| θησόμενος | θησομένη | θησόμενον |

Aorist (without augment):

| σάμενος | σαμένη | σάμενον |
| θείς | θεῖσα | θέν |

Perfect (with reduplication—see para. 115 (e)):

| μένος | μένη | μένον |

The relationship between these tenses should be noted here
again, as throughout the verb, to assist the memory in recognizing the various forms. The fut. mid. is formed from the pres.
by the insertion of σ before the terminations of the latter, then
the fut. pass. from this by the further insertion of the element
θη. The perf. also follows the pres., with omission of the
connecting vowel o (note accent in masc. and neut. forms).

The mascs. and neuts. in os and ov are declined regularly as of the 2nd decl. (para. 19 (*a*) and (*b*)), and the fems. in η like γραφή (para. 18 (*a*)). The aor. pass. fem. is declined like βασίλισσα (para. 18 (*b*)). The stem of the aor. masc. and neut. passives is θεντ, and the form is declined as a dental after the model of the 3rd decl., model **c** (para. 77); the neut. pl. is θέντα in accordance with rule (para. 17 (iii)).

The syntactical principles are, of course, the same as for the active voice (paras. 143–149).

185. As indicated in para. 169, the 3rd pers. pl. of the perfs. pass. is formed analytically, or periphrastically, being made up of the pass. part. and εἰμί used as an auxiliary verb; these forms can now be seen. 'They have been written' cannot be expressed in Greek synthetically, so the only possible form is εἰσι γεγραμμένοι (or -αι or -α, according to the gender of the subject of the finite verb). The exact force of the Greek pres.-perf. can here be felt; the above form really means 'they are having been written' = 'they are written', and such is the true English equivalent of the form. The past-perf. ('they had been written') would be ἦσαν γεγραμμένοι.

186. The student is now in possession of all the terminations of Greek verbs of the 1st, or ω, conj.; there are, therefore, no more of these to be learnt. There are a few adjectives formed directly from some verbs—διδακτός (taught, instructed), fr. διδάσκω (see para. 179); but these stand apart from the conjugation of the verb strictly considered.

EXERCISE 24

Give English for:

μὴ ἰσχυρότεροι τοῦ Κυρίου ἐσμεν; τὸ μωρὸν τοῦ Θεοῦ σοφώτερον τῶν ἀνθρώπων ἐστιν, καὶ τὸ ἀσθενὲς τοῦ Θεοῦ ἰσχυρότερον τῶν ἀνθρώπων. τὰ μέγιστα καὶ τίμια ἐπαγγέλματα. τὸν πρῶτον λόγον ἐποιησάμην, κράτιστε Θεόφιλε.

χαρὰ ἐν οὐρανῷ ἔσται ἐπὶ ἑνὶ ἁμαρτωλῷ μετανοοῦντι ἢ ἐπὶ
ἐνενήκοντα ἐννέα δικαίοις οἵτινες οὐ χρείαν ἔχουσιν μετανοίας.
μείζων ὁ προφητεύων ἢ ὁ λαλῶν γλώσσαις. νῦν ἐγγύτερον
ἡμῶν ἡ σωτηρία ἢ ὅτε ἐπιστεύσαμεν. ἔχομεν βεβαιότερον τὸν
προφητικὸν λόγον. ὁ τε γὰρ ἁγιάζων καὶ οἱ ἁγιαζόμενοι ἐξ
ἑνὸς πάντες. ἦν ὁ υἱὸς αὐτοῦ ὁ πρεσβύτερος ἐν ἀγρῷ. οὐκέτι
εἰμὶ ἄξιος κληθῆναι υἱός σου· ποιησόν με ὡς ἕνα τῶν μισθίων
σου. μείζων ἐστὶν ὁ ἐν ὑμῖν ἢ ὁ ἐν τῷ κόσμῳ. πᾶς ὁ
πιστεύων ὅτι Ἰησοῦς ἐστιν ὁ χριστὸς ἐκ τοῦ Θεοῦ γεγέννηται·
καὶ πᾶς ὁ ἀγαπῶν τὸν γεννήσαντα ἀγαπᾷ τὸν γεγεννημένον ἐξ
αὐτοῦ.

ALTERNATIVE TENSE FORMS

187. While it is true—as stated in para. 186—that there are no
other *terminations* to be learnt for any verbs of the 1st conj.,
into the remaining six classes of verbs yet to be studied a
complication enters, in that some of them have alternative
tense *forms*, while others vary the spelling of their stems. In
these respects they differ from those already considered, in
which the stem is unaltered throughout, save for a few simple
exceptions, and only one form can occur for any particular
meaning. The subject has its difficulties, but the line of
approach now taken to this feature of the Greek verb will, we
think, make its mastery as simple as possible.

The position may be illustrated, to some extent, from English
usage. There are in English two ways of forming the simple
past tense ('past indefinite' as distinct from 'past continuous')
of verbs, known as the 'weak' and the 'strong' formation.
The former consists in the addition of *ed* (or *t*) to the present—
as 'I jump', 'I jumped'. The latter is when the vowel of the
present is modified for the past, without any addition to the
verb—as 'I sing', 'I sang'. Verbs forming their past in one
way do not as a rule have the other formation as well—a verb
is conjugated one way or the other, and, knowing our mother

tongue, we know which. In the very few verbs in which two past tense forms do exist side by side (*e.g.*, from 'hang', 'hanged' and 'hung'), there is a slight but real difference of usage between the two forms.

Something like this now confronts us in Greek. We find verbs with a 'second aorist', a 'second future', and a 'second perfect'; but the term 'second' does not imply any numerical order, except that these forms are generally learnt after the first. Some grammarians, indeed, favour the terms 'weak' and 'strong aorist', etc., as used above in English; these have something to recommend them on the score of grammatical appropriateness, but are cumbersome, and '1st aor.' and '2nd aor.' do very well to indicate these alternative tense forms, as we have called them.

In Greek also, with some exceptions, if a verb has secondary tenses it does not have the first as well. Where the two forms exist side by side it is with a difference of meaning; otherwise the secondary tenses have the same meaning as the first would have if they existed.

The first, or primary, tenses are of course those that have been so far learnt.

The rules for conjugating these secondary tenses are quite simple, as follows.

SECOND AORIST

188. Active and middle voices—in the indicative mood, the terminations of the imperfect are added to the 2nd aor. stem (see below); in all other moods, the terminations of the present.

Passive voice—the same endings are used as for 1st aor., but omitting the initial θ which is characteristic of the latter.

SECOND FUTURE

189. This occurs in the passive voice only, and is related to the first future just as the two aorist passives are connected—that is, omitting the θ, and using the same 2nd aor. stem.

SECOND PERFECTS

190. These occur in the active voice only; the terminations are the same as in the first perfects, but omitting κ, just as θ is for the 2nd aor. and 2nd fut. passives. Second perfects are found occasionally only, and the stem is then sometimes modified, with change of meaning.

It is impossible to say more by way of general principles for these alternative tense forms; verbs in which they occur must be studied more or less in detail. Euphony has something to say in deciding whether primary or secondary tenses are used, and a verb may have a 1st aor. act. and a 2nd aor. pass., and *vice versa*.

A so-called 3rd fut. (really a fut.-perf.—see para. 115) occurs once only in T.R., but, for the reason given, is ignored here.

VERBS: CONSONANT STEMS
Class B 5

191. In contrast with B 3 verbs, with their short stem vowel, there are those whose stem, in their lexical form, consists of a long monosyllable. It is this stem which appears unchanged in the present and imperfect tenses; while the 2nd aor. and 2nd fut. modify it to a short stem. Common verbs of this class are $\phi\epsilon\acute{u}\gamma\omega$ (I flee) and $\lambda\epsilon\acute{\iota}\pi\omega$ (I leave), with, of course, their compounds. The secondary stems of these being respectively $\phi\upsilon\gamma$ and $\lambda\iota\pi$, their conjugation presents no difficulty; thus—

> 2nd aor. act. ind., $\emph{ἔφυγον}$, $\emph{ἔλιπον}$
>   subj., $\phi\acute{u}\gamma\omega$, $\lambda\acute{\iota}\pi\omega$
>   part., $\phi\upsilon\gamma\acute{\omega}\nu$, $\lambda\iota\pi\acute{\omega}\nu$ (note accent)
>   inf., $\phi\upsilon\gamma\epsilon\widehat{\iota}\nu$, $\lambda\iota\pi\epsilon\widehat{\iota}\nu$ (note accent)

2nd aor. mid. ind., ἐφυγόμην, ἐλιπόμην

inf., φυγέσθαι, λιπέσθαι

2nd aor. pass. ind., ἐθύγην, ἐλίπην

2nd fut. pass. ind., φυγήσεται, λιπήσεται

In the 2nd aor. pass. there is one departure only from rule; this is that in the 2nd pers. sing. of the imperative the termination is ηθι instead of (θ)ητι. Thus—φύγηθι, λίπηθι. Otherwise the tenses not given above are formed in strict analogy with the forms set out, in all persons and numbers.

VOCABULARY

192. ἄγω (I lead), though a short monosyllabic stem of class B 3, does have a 2nd aor.: ind. ἤγαγον, subj. ἀγάγω, inf. ἀγαγεῖν, etc.; that is, the stem is doubled, with the temporal augment, η for α, in the ind. The hortatory subjunctive, ἄγωμεν, has the special meaning 'let us go'.

ἔχω also has a 2nd aor.: ind. ἔσχον. Its imperf. is εἶχον, and its pres.-perf. ἔσχηκα.

πείθω (I persuade), again, though a dental belonging to class B 4, has a 2nd aor. stem πιθ, and a 2nd perf. with special meaning—πέποιθα (I trust).

EXERCISE 25

Give English for:

φευγέτωσαν εἰς τὰ ὄρη. οὐ μὴ ἐκφύγωσιν. πάντες ἔφυγον. εἴ τις ὑμῶν λείπεται σοφίας, αἰτείτω παρὰ Θεοῦ. ἐγὼ ἐδεήθην περὶ σοῦ ἵνα μὴ ἐκλίπῃ ἡ πίστις σου. ἄγωμεν ἐντεῦθεν. συνάξει τὸν σῖτον αὐτοῦ εἰς τὴν ἀποθήκην, τὸ δὲ ἄχυρον κατακαύσει πυρὶ ἀσβέστῳ. συναγάγετε τὰ περισσεύσαντα κλάσματα. ἕξεις θησαυρὸν ἐν οὐρανῷ. ἦσαν λαμπάδες ἱκαναὶ ἐν τῷ ὑπερῴῳ οὗ ἦμεν συνηγμένοι. εἶχον αὐτοὶ ἰχθύδια ὀλίγα. εἶχε τὸ θυγάτριον αὐτῆς πνεῦμα ἀκάθαρτον.

CONSONANT STEMS

Class B 6

193. Many labial stems are modified from their true form—seen in cognate nouns—by the addition of τ in the pres. tenses. As τ is a sharp mute (see para. 10), the consonant preceding it must be sharp; but that consonant may, in the original stem, be a sharp, a flat, or an aspirate. Examples of each, respectively, are—

> τύπτω (stem—τυπ) (I strike)
> κρύπτω (κρυβ) (I hide)
> θάπτω (ταφ) (I bury)

The true stem of the first of these is seen in the cognate noun τύπος (mark, impression). In the last, the aspirate (φ) of the stem is lost when the τ is added, so the initial τ becomes θ by way of compensation, as happens in some other verbs. The true stem of this verb is seen in τάφος (a tomb) (cp. Eng. epi*taph*).

The fut. is formed regularly from the true stem of these verbs—τύψω, κρύψω, θάψω, etc.; and the τ of the pres. is disregarded for the other tenses also, conjugation proceeding in accordance with rule (para. 176). But these verbs commonly, though not always, have 2nd aor. tenses—which, in the ind. act., would be, for the above verbs respectively, ἔτυπον, ἔκρυβον, ἔταφον. As a matter of fact, however, κρύπτω is an example of a verb having a 1st aor. act. and a 2nd aor. pass.—ἔκρυψα, ἐκρύβην.

Γίνομαι (I become)

194. This is such a common verb, and its meaning so special, as to call for separate treatment. Though having a liquid stem, and so belonging to class B 10, it presents no peculiar difficulties, and, now that deponents and alternative tenses have been studied, it can be disposed of.

To begin with, γίνομαι must be carefully distinguished from two other verbs. Εἰμί (paras. 39–41, 154–158) is the true substantive verb, etymologically related to the Lat. *sum*, and connoting the fact of existence; it is regularly used also as an auxiliary verb. Ὑπάρχω also means 'I am', 'I subsist', but with a difference in usage from εἰμί.

The verb now before us, on the other hand, denotes the coming into existence of what did not exist before, the becoming of something different from what it was before, or the happening of events. It is used of the water becoming wine (John 2. 9) and in the temptation that stones should become loaves (Mat. 4. 3); and it is regularly used of the Incarnation (John 1. 14, Gal. 4. 4, *et al.*). This verb is therefore not used of God, save as He is relatively to the creature, as in Heb. 11. 6). While the verb must often be rendered as though it were equivalent to εἰμί, English idiom not always allowing the use of 'become', the tendency—seen in A.V.—to treat it as the same as the passive of ποιέω must be resisted. The discrimination between εἰμί and γίνομαι is one of the most fruitful subjects of N.T. study, and the student should never ignore it.

Example:
πρὶν Ἀβραὰμ γενέσθαι ἐγὼ εἰμί (John 8. 58)
= before Abraham was (*lit.* came into being) I am

The prologue to John's gospel may be studied for further easily apprehended examples.

The original stem of γίνομαι, seen in 2nd aor., etc., was γεν, with a kind of reduplication γι, making γιγεν; this became shortened to γιγν, and then to γιν, which is the pres. stem with which we have to do in N.T. It is a deponent verb (para. 172). The form ἐγένετο (it came to pass), so frequent in the gospels, is, then, the 3rd pers. sing. 2nd aor. ind. Matthew's phrase, incidentally, is the Hebraistic καὶ ἐγένετο, Luke's the more classical ἐγένετο δέ. All the tenses of this verb are regularly formed, though η may be inserted after the stem as a connecting vowel: fut. ind. γενήσομαι, 1st aor. ἐγενήθην, pres.-perf. γεγένημαι. There is a 2nd perf.—γέγονα (τὸ γεγονός, that which, or what, has happened). The 3rd pers. sing. of the 2nd aor. opt. is used by Paul—μὴ γένοιτο (may it not be).

VOCABULARY

195. Nearly all B 6 verbs have labial stems; but one important guttural (there are no dentals) falls within its limits—τίκτω (I bear [a child]). The stem of this is τεκ (cp. τέκνον, a child); hence 2nd aor. ind. act. ἔτεκον, 1st aor. pass. ἐτέχθην, fut. (mid. with act. meaning) τέξομαι.

πίπτω (I fall) calls for special attention, as, though apparently doing so, it does not belong to this B 6 clas. Its stem is πετ, increased (cp. γίνομαι) to πιπετ, then shortened to πιπτ. The τ, however, is softened to σ in conjugating; hence 2nd aor. ind. act. ἔπεσον, inf. πεσεῖν, part. πεσών; but pres.-perf. πέπτωκα.

EXERCISE 26

Give English for:

μετὰ δὲ ταῦτα ἠρώτησεν τὸν Πειλᾶτον Ἰωσὴφ ἀπὸ Ἀριμαθαίας, ὧν μαθητὴς Ἰησοῦ κεκρυμμένος δὲ διὰ τὸν φόβον τῶν Ἰουδαίων. ἔκρυψα τὸ τάλαντόν σου ἐν τῇ γῇ. ἡ ζωὴ ὑμῶν κέκρυπται σὺν τῷ χριστῷ ἐν τῷ θεῷ. ὁ λόγος σὰρξ ἐγένετο καὶ ἐσκήνωσεν ἐν ὑμῖν. πεσόντες προσεκύνησαν οἱ μάγοι τῷ παιδίῳ Ἰησοῦ. ἡ οἰκία ἔπεσεν, καὶ ἦν ἡ πτῶσις αὐτῆς μεγάλη. πέσετε ἐφ᾽ ἡμᾶς. βλεπέτω μὴ πέσῃ. ἡ ἀγάπη οὐδέποτε πίπτει. γενηθήτω τὸ θέλημά σου. ὁ πρῶτος ἄγγελος ἐσάλπισεν. ἔβλεψα ἀστέρα ἐκ τοῦ οὐρανοῦ πεπτωκότα εἰς τὴν γῆν. ὡς ἐπίστευσας γενηθήτω σοι. ὁ Θεὸς τοῖς ἐκζητοῦσιν αὐτὸν μισθαποδότης γίνεται.

CONJUNCTIONS

196. Conjunctions join not only single words, but also

sentences; and to construe these latter correctly it is necessary to distinguish between conjunctions which (1) *co*-ordinate two or more sentences and those which (2) *sub*ordinate one sentence to another.

(1) Conjunctions such as καί, ἀλλά, and δέ co-ordinate sentences of equal value, so to speak.

Example:

> ἀργύριον καὶ χρυσίον οὐχ ὑπάρχει μοι, ὃ δὲ ἔχω τοῦτό σοι δίδωμι (Acts 3. 6)
> = I have no silver and gold, but what I have this I give thee

These two sentences are independent of each other, and each gives a complete sense without the other; they are co-ordinate sentences. The verbs in the two sentences are in the same mood—indicative, because it is a question of stating facts.

(2) Conjunctions such as ἵνα subordinate; one sentence, incomplete in sense in itself, depends on another, the principal sentence, for its full force, and here will be seen to come in one of the functions of the subjunctive and optative moods (see Rule 14, para. 170).

Example:

> ὁ κλέπτης οὐκ ἔρχεται εἰ μὴ ἵνα κλέψῃ καὶ θύσῃ καὶ ἀπολέσῃ (John 10. 10)
> = the thief comes not except that he may steal and kill and destroy

The strict rule for the determination of the mood in subordinate sentences is this: If the principal sentence has its verb in a primary tense (para. 140) the subj. mood must be used in the dependent sentence; whereas if the principal sentence contains an historic tense the opt. mood must be used in the subordinate sentence. But this rule is a literary refinement not always observed in N.T., and therefore we do not formally state it here; it will be sufficient, for the most part, if the student recognizes the general distinction between the ind. and subj. moods. Roughly, that between the subj. and the opt. is as 'may' is to 'might' respectively.

But it has also to be considered, in deciding the mood to be used after conjunctions which subordinate one sentence to another, whether the subordinated sentence is—(a) categorical or definite, or (b) hypothetical or indefinite.

Examples:

(a) ὅτε ἤνοιξεν τὸ ἀρνίον μίαν ἐκ τῶν ἑπτὰ σφραγίδων (Rev. 6. 1)
   = when the Lamb opened one of the seven seals

(b) ὅταν δὲ πάλιν εἰσαγάγῃ τὸν πρωτότοκον εἰς τὴν οἰκου-μένην, λέγει (Heb. 1. 6)
   = and whenever he again brings in the firstborn into the world, he says

When the dependent sentence is quite definite, as in (a), alluding to a known fact, the verb is in the ind. mood; but when, as in (b), something hypothetical is in mind (and ἄν always suggests this) the subj. is used—though there are exceptions.

Co-ordinating Conjunctions

197. Those marked with an asterisk are post-positive (cp. Rule 16, para. 178). The compound forms may be found either as one word, hyphenated, or as separate words.

ἀλλά (used very like πλήν, nevertheless, etc.), but, except; ἀλλ' ἤ, except
γάρ,* for
δέ,* but, and, now, so, on the other hand (not so strong as ἀλλά); see μέν
ἤ. or

καί, and; sometimes modifying a following word—'even'; καίτοι, καίτοιγε, and yet

μέν*; not always translatable, generally balanced by δέ, sometimes by ἀλλά or πλήν, each of the two introducing a clause intended to be contrasted with the other— 'indeed ... but'; μὲν οὖν, μὲν οὖνγε, nay more, nay rather; μέντοι, indeed, really

οὐδέ, not even, nor

οὖν,* therefore, then, so; οὐκοῦν, not really?

οὔτε ... οὔτε, neither ... nor

τε,* and; weaker than καί; τε ... τε, or καί, or δέ, τε καί, both ... and

τοιγαροῦν, accordingly, wherefore; τοίνυν,* so

Subordinating Conjunctions

198.

ἄχρι(ς), until

διότι (= διὰ ὅ τι), wherefore, because

ἐάν (= εἰ ἄν), εἰ, if

εἴτε ... εἴτε, whether ... or

ἐπεί, ἐπειδή, ἐπειδήπερ, when, after that, since

ἕως, until

ἵνα, in order that

καίπερ, though

μέχρι(ς), as far as, until

μή, lest

ὁπότε, ὅτε, when

ὅπως, so that

ὅταν (= ὅτε ἄν), whenever, whensoever

ὅτι, that (in direct statement)

πρίν, before

ὥστε, so as to (twice only in N.T. with ind., otherwise with inf.)

VERBS: CONSONANT STEMS

Class B 7

199. This class is of the form ἁμαρτάνω (I sin). The stem of this verb is ἁμαρτ (cp. ἁμαρτία), and the element αν is a modifying addition, confined, of course, to the pres. and imperf. tenses. These verbs may have a further modification, as shown in the vocabulary below—which, as there are not many such verbs, is all but, if not quite, complete. The 2nd aor. ind. of ἁμαρτάνω is, naturally, ἥμαρτον. The futures and perfects of these verbs must be studied individually as they do not conform to any one rule; the fut. ind. of ἁμαρτάνω is ἁμαρτήσω, and the pres.-perf. ἡμάρτηκα.

200. Rule 17. *Verbs and adjectives indicating a mental attitude commonly take the dative case.*

Example:

τὰ τέκνα, ὑπακούετε τοῖς γονεῦσιν ὑμῶν (Eph. 6. 1)
= children, obey ye your parents
Fr. = enfants, obéissez à vos parents
(Cp. Acts 7. 39; Rom. 6. 16)

VOCABULARY

201. *Class B 7 verbs:* αὐξάνω, stem—αὐξ, I grow; 1st aor. ηὔξησα. βλαστάνω, stem—βλαστ, I sprout; 1st aor. ἐβλάστησα. θιγγάνω, stem—θιγ, I touch; 2nd aor. ἔθιγον. λαγχάνω, stem—λαχ, I obtain; 2nd aor. ἔλαχον. λαμβάνω, stem—λαβ, I receive; 2nd aor. ἔλαβον, but fut. λήψομαι or λήμψομαι; pres.-perf. εἴληφα. λανθάνω, stem—λαθ, I am hidden; 2nd aor. ἔλαθον. μανθάνω, stem—μαθ, I learn (cp. μαθητής); 2nd aor. ἔμαθον. πυνθάνομαι, stem—πυθ, I inquire; 2nd aor. ἐπυθόμην. τυγχάνω, stem—τυχ, I chance; fut. τεύξομαι, 2nd aor. ἔτυχον.

EXERCISE 27

Give English for:

οὐδενὶ δεδουλεύκαμεν πώποτε. πάντες γὰρ ἥμαρτον καὶ
ὑστεροῦνται τῆς δόξης τοῦ Θεοῦ. διὰ τῆς ἀγάπης δουλεύετε
ἀλλήλοις. μάθετε ἀπ᾽ ἐμοῦ. τοῦτο μόνον θέλω μαθεῖν ἀφ᾽
ὑμῶν, ἐξ ἔργων νόμου τὸ πνεῦμα ἐλάβετε ἢ ἐξ ἀκοῆς πίστεως;
ὅσοι δὲ ἔλαβον αὐτὸν ἐγένοντο τέκνα Θεοῦ. τὸ πνεῦμα τῆς
ἀληθείας ἐμὲ δοξάσει, ὅτι ἐκ τοῦ ἐμοῦ λήμψεται. ὁμοία ἐστὶν
ἡ βασιλεία τῶν οὐρανῶν ζύμῃ, ἣν λαβοῦσα γυνὴ ἐνέκρυψεν εἰς
ἀλεύρου σάτα τρία ἕως οὗ ἐζυμώθη ὅλον. μὴ ἅψῃ μηδὲ γεύσῃ
μηδὲ θίγῃς.

IMPROPER PREPOSITIONS

202. In para. 168 a complete list of 'proper' prepositions was
given. All other prepositions are called 'improper', and
cannot be used in composition with verbs, as the former can
and are. They nearly all govern the genitive case. They are
really adverbs, or of adverbial origin, while adverbs themselves
are or may be derived from the oblique cases of nouns. When
the word 'preposition' is used it is often taken as covering only
the eighteen proper prepositions, though of course any word so
'placed before' a noun is a preposition.

Below is a complete list of the improper prepositions. It
will be noticed that some appeared in the list of conjunctions;
this is because the same word is differently classified according
to its function; cp. English 'that'—either a demonstrative
adjective, a relative pronoun, or a conjunction.

ἅμα (dat.), together with
ἄνευ, without
ἄχρι(ς), until
ἐγγύς (dat. sometimes), near—time or space
ἔμπροσθεν, before
ἐναντίον, in front of, against, opposite
ἕνεκα or ἕνεκεν, for the sake of

ἐνώπιον, before, in the presence of
ἔξω, without = outside
ἐπάνω, above
ἔσω, within
ἕως, as far as
μέσον, in the midst of
μεταξύ, between
μέχρι(ς), until
ὀπίσω, ὄπισθεν, behind, after
ὀψέ, at the end of
πλήν, except
πλησίον, near; παραπλήσιον (dat.), very near
ὑπερέκεινα, beyond
χάριν, by favour of, for the sake of
χώρις, without, apart from

Some of these are synonymous, or nearly so.   C. J. Vaughan
says, on Heb. 4. 12: 'The two forms, μέχρι (μακρός), *to the
length of*, and ἄχρι (ἄκρος), *to the extremity of*, occur often in
N.T., and apparently with no difference of meaning; for we
have ἄχρι θανάτου in Acts 22. 4, Rev. 2. 10, 12. 11, and μέχρι
θανάτου in Phil. 2. 8, and μέχρις αἵματος in Heb. 12. 4.'

VERBS: CONSONANT STEMS
Class B 8

203. Here again is a sharply defined class of Greek verbs, the
distinguishing feature of which is the element σκ appearing in
the present stem.   This is absent in the other tenses, just as
with αν in B 7 verbs.   Caution, however, is necessary here, as
not all -σκω verbs do in fact belong to this class.   For example,
βόσκω (I feed or tend) is rather a B 3 verb, but as it occurs in
N.T. only in the pres. no further remarks are called for here.
Again, διδάσκω belongs to the B 3 class, and has been already
disposed of (para. 179).   Otherwise, the vocabulary in para.

204 gives the verbs of this class, with the formation of the other tenses. They vary somewhat in form, but fall into two subclasses—vowel and consonant.

Original vowel stems add σκ directly, with, in some verbs, lengthening of a short stem vowel. So θνα, formed by metathesis from θαν.

Original consonant stems add ισκ, and often have a related stem in ε. So εὑρ or εὑρε.

These verbs are sometimes called 'inchoate', because many of them include the idea of the beginning of an action, indicated by the element σκ, represented in similar verbs in Lat. by *sc*.

VOCABULARY

204. The vocabulary of these B 8 verbs must be somewhat more detailed. Some of them have the ι reduplication in the pres. like γίνομαι.

ἀποθνήσκω—see θνήσκω below.

ἀρέσκω (stem—ἀρε), I please (taking the dat. as in Fr.); fut. ἀρέσω, 1st aor. ἤρεσα.

γινώσκω (for γιγνώσκω) (γνο), come to know, learn; fut. γνώσομαι, 1st aor. ἔγνωσα, 2nd aor. ἔγνων, pres.-perf. ἔγνωκα = I (now) know. There are a few important compounds.

θνήσκω (θαν)—only in composition, ἀποθνήσκω, I die; 2nd aor. ἀπέθανον, pres.-perf. ἀποτέθνηκα.

ἱλάσκομαι, I am propitious *or* merciful to (c. dat.); 1st aor. ἱλάσθην.

μιμνήσκομαι (μνα), I remember (c. gen.—cp. Eng. 'to be mindful of' something); 1st aor. ἐμνήσθην, pres.-perf. μέμνημαι.

πιπράσκω, I sell; 1st aor. pass. ἐπράθην, pres.-perf. act. πέπρακα, pres.-perf. pass. πέπραμαι.

EXERCISE 28

Give English for:

ἐκέλευσεν αὐτὸν ὁ κύριος πραθῆναι καὶ τὴν γυναῖκα καὶ τὰ

τέκνα καὶ πάντα ὅσα ἔχει. ἐγὼ δὲ σάρκινός εἰμι, πεπραμένος
ὑπὸ τὴν ἁμαρτίαν. ὁ Θεός, ἱλάσθητί μοι. ἕκαστος ὑμῶν τῷ
πλησίον ἀρεσκέτω εἰς τὸ ἀγαθὸν πρὸς οἰκοδόμην. οὐ ζητῶ
ἀνθρώποις ἀρέσκειν. οὐδεὶς ἐπιγινώσκει τὸν υἱὸν εἰ μὴ ὁ
πατήρ. ὁ κόσμος δι' αὐτοῦ ἐγένετο, καὶ ὁ κόσμος αὐτὸν οὐκ
ἔγνω. γινώσκεις ἃ ἀναγινώσκεις; οὐ γάρ ἐστιν κρυπτὸν ὃ οὐ
φανερὸν γενήσεται, οὐδὲ ἀπόκρυφον ὃ οὐ γνωσθήσεται.
μιμνήσκεσθε τῶν δεσμῶν μου. ὁ ἀναγινώσκων νοείτω.
τοῦτον οὖν τὸν τίτλον πολλοὶ ἀνέγνωσαν τῶν Ἰουδαίων.

DIRECT AND INDIRECT STATEMENTS

205. It is necessary to understand these two constructions, in
Greek and English, as otherwise the student will be perplexed
by the change of tense in the verb due to the fact that the idioms
of the two languages are not identical. An example of each
construction in English will show what is involved.

Direct: He said, 'I am a prophet'.

Indirect: He said that he was a prophet.

In the former (*oratio recta*) the words actually used by the
speaker are reproduced, our modern system of punctuation
including these in quotation marks. In the latter (*oratio
obliqua*) the actual words are not given, but the statement made
is reproduced indirectly, the tense of the verb is altered to suit
that of the introductory sentence ('sequence of tenses'), the
1st pers. pron. is made into the 3rd, and the two sentences
joined by the conjunction 'that' ('recitative *that*').

The Greek idiom is different. ὅτι (that) is often, though
not always, used to introduce the exact words uttered by the
original speaker, and is, therefore, according to our mode of
expression, redundant; in fact, it must be omitted in rendering
into English. The pronoun and the tense of the verb remain
unchanged. Greek had no quotation marks, and ὅτι, thus

employed, did duty therefor—indeed, it has been facetiously
said that ὅτι is 'Greek for "quotation marks"'.

Example:

> ἔτι αὐτοῦ λαλοῦντος ἔρχεταί τις παρὰ τοῦ ἀρχισυναγώγου
> λέγων ὅτι Τέθνηκεν ἡ θυγάτηρ σου (Luke 8. 49)
> = as he was yet speaking, one comes from the ruler of the
> synagogue, saying, 'Thy daughter is dead'

The same principle holds good when it is a question of
reporting incidents—Greek retains the tense which was
appropriate at the time of the occurrence, whereas in English
we alter it to suit that of the report.

Example:

> ἐκεῖνοι δὲ ἔδοξαν ὅτι περὶ τῆς κοιμήσεως τοῦ ὕπνου λέγει
> (John 11. 13)
> = but they thought that he was speaking with reference
> to the rest of sleep

Other passages which will repay study in this respect are
Mat. 2. 22, John 10. 34, 36, 11. 13, Acts 12. 9.

VERBS: CONSONANT STEMS

Class B 9

206. A few verbs have a guttural stem ending, softened to an
σ or τ sound for the pres. and imperf. tenses. Cognate nouns
and adjectives will afford a clue to the true stem, seen in the
other tenses, of these verbs. Thus—

> φυλάσσω (φυλακ; cp. φυλακή, φύλαξ), guard

The original modification of these stems, and of such a verb
as κράζω (para. 181), was by the insertion of a short vowel
(ι or ε) after the stem; and the softening thus occasioned may

be compared to the effect of *i* on *t* in the common English syllable *-tion*. Geldart (*The Modern Greek Language in its Relation to Ancient Greek*) says: 'διατάζω, the modern Greek and most ancient form, as I believe, of διατάσσω, must have passed through the following stages: διαταγέω (I am a διαταγός), διατάγιω, διατάγjω, διατάζω, διατάσσω.'

VOCABULARY

207. *B 9 Verbs*: κηρύσσω (stem—κηρυκ; cp. κῆρυξ, a herald, κήρυγμα, a proclamation), I proclaim, preach, herald; πλήσσω (πληγ; cp. πληγή, a stroke, πλήκτης, a striker), I strike; πράσσω (πρακ; cp. Eng. *practise*; πρᾶγμα, a thing done, πρᾶξις, an action), I do, act; ταράσσω (ταραχ; cp. ταραχή, a disturbance, also τάραχος), I disturb, trouble; τάσσω (ταγ; cp. τάξις, an arrangement), I order, constitute, arrange. All these verbs form their aorists, futures, and perfects regularly as from a guttural stem (para. 176).

πλάσσω (I mould, form), however, has πλάσω for fut., its stem being πλας (cp. πλάσμα, a thing formed *or* fashioned, πλαστός, adj., formed).

ἀνοίγω (I open; ἀνά + οἴγω, but the simple verb οἴγω does not occur) has three different augments for the aor. pass.: ἀνεῴχθη and ἠνεῴχθη (1st aor.) and ἠνοίγη (2nd aor.). In the first there is the insertion of ε between preposition and verb, with lengthening of οι to ῳ, and in the second form initial α is lengthened to η as well. A 2nd fut. pass. also occurs.

πάσχω, I suffer, has a 2nd aor. stem παθ (cp. πάθημα suffering, also πάθος emotion, and adj. παθητός, destined to suffer).

μέλλω (I am about [to do something]) is an interesting verb; it nearly always conveys the notion of imminence, while sometimes it is difficult to discern more than simple futurity. It must always be followed by a verb in the infinitive, showing what is about to be done.

EXERCISE 29

Give English for:

οὗτος δὲ οὐδὲν ἄτοπον ἔπραξεν. μὴ ταρασσέσθω ὑμῶν ἡ
καρδία μηδὲ δειλιάτω. κύριε, ἄνοιξον ὑμῖν. ταῦτα (para. 7)
πράσσεις. Ἀδὰμ γὰρ πρῶτος ἐπλάσθη, εἶτα Εὔα. τί μέλλετε
πράσσειν; Ἰησοῦ, μνήσθητί μου. Χριστὸς ἔπαθεν ὑπὲρ
ἡμῶν. κρούετε, καὶ ἀνοιγήσεται ὑμῖν. ὁ μισῶν τὴν ψυχὴν
αὐτοῦ ἐν τῷ κόσμῳ τούτῳ εἰς ζωὴν αἰώνιον φυλάξει αὐτήν.
καίπερ ὢν υἱός, ἔμαθεν ἀφ' ὧν ἔπαθεν τὴν ὑπακοήν. διδάσκαλε, ταῦτα πάντα ἐφυλαξάμην ἐκ νεότητός μου. ἤκουσα
ἄγγελον ἰσχυρὸν κηρύσσοντα ἐν φωνῇ μεγάλῃ.

CONSONANT STEMS

Class B 10

208. All that now remains of verbs of the 1st conj. (apart
from any calling for special consideration) is the fairly large
class of liquid verbs—*i.e.*, those whose stem ends in λ, μ, ν, or
ρ (para. 9).

The most striking feature in the conjugation of these verbs
occurs in the fut. tenses. σ, which is characteristic of the fut.
terminations in all moods, etc., cannot immediately follow a
liquid; hence the following steps are taken in conjugating these
verbs in their tenses. First, ε is inserted between the stem and
the fut. ending; then the σ drops out from between the two
vowels; lastly, contraction ensues between the vowels thus
brought together. Taking a common N.T. verb of this class,
we have, therefore—

κρίνω, I judge
(κρινέσω, κρινέω) κρινῶ, I shall judge

For practical purposes, then, it may be taken that a liquid verb
is conjugated in its fut. tenses like an A 2 verb in ε in its pres.
tenses, with normal contraction according to the table in para.

151. The only difference between the two forms above given (pres. and fut.) lies in the accentuation, as can be seen at a glance.

While there are no modifications in the stem of κρίνω, there are modified stems in some liquid verbs—e.g., double λ may occur in the pres. only. Thus—

> βάλλω, I throw, cast
> βαλῶ, I shall throw
> ἔβαλον (2nd aor.), I threw

Or the modified vowel of the pres. is restored (cp. φεύγω, φυγ). Thus—

> φαίνω, I shine
> φανῶ, I shall shine

In the 1st aor., the σ is dropped in the act. and mid. (ἔκρινα, ἐκρινάμην), and in the pass. the ν is dropped (ἐκρίθην).

In the perf. act., as μ and ν cannot come before κ, various expedients are adopted. κρίνω, κλίνω (I bow), and πλύνω (I wash), drop the ν (κέκρινα, etc.). Other verbs, as φαίνω, which has ἔφηνα for its 1st aor., adopt a 2nd perf. from the same modified stem (πέφηνα). μένω (I remain) makes its perf. as though from an ε stem—μεμένηκα.

In the perf. pass., ν is changed into σ or μ before μαι, as πέφασμαι instead of πε-φαν-μαι; from ξηραίνω (I dry up), ἐξήραμμαι for ἐ-ξηραν-μαι. But if a verb drops the ν for the perf. act., it does so also in the mid.-pass., as κέκριμαι; and a verb which assumes a root in ε for the perf. act. constructs the pass. and all its aorists similarly.

Verbs of class B 7 of the form μανθάνω must not be confused with verbs of this class with stem ending in ν, the true stem of μανθάνω, for instance, being μαθ, as has been shown.

209. In some other verbs, moreover, the ν is no part of the

true stem—*e.g.* πίνω (I drink; stem—πι), fut. πίομαι; φθάνω (I anticipate; φθα), fut. φθάσω; κάμνω (I am weary; καμ); δάκνω (I bite; δακ); ἐλαύνω (I drive; ἐλα); βαίνω (I go; βα). The last occurs in N.T. only in composition, but very frequently thus; the α lengthens to η—2nd aor. ἔβην, fut. βήσομαι.

EXERCISE 30

Give English for:

ἔπλυναν τὰς στολὰς αὐτῶν καὶ ἐλεύκαναν αὐτὰς ἐν τῷ αἵματι τοῦ ἀρνίου. ἔπλυνον τὰ δίκτυα αὐτῶν. βάλε σεαυτὸν κάτω. ἡ δὲ ἡμέρα ἤρξατο κλίνειν. ἡ τελεία ἀγάπη ἔξω βάλλει τὸν φόβον. μὴ κρίνετε, ἵνα μὴ κριθῆτε. ἔρχεται Μαριὰμ ἡ Μαγδαληνὴ ἀγγέλλουσα τοῖς μαθηταῖς ὅτι ἑώρακα τὸν κύριον. μεῖνον μεθ᾽ ἡμῶν, ὅτι πρὸς ἑσπέραν ἐστὶ καὶ κέκλινεν ἤδη ἡ ἡμέρα.

IMPERSONAL VERBS

210. There are a number of verbs called 'impersonal', because they are used only in the 3rd pers. sing., with the meaning in English of 'it is (*or* was, etc.) . . .' In all languages there are some notions which cannot be associated with personal action strictly so called—'it rains', and so on (though in this instance the Greeks may have thought of Zeus as the subject of the verb, βρέχει); and while the usages of various languages differ in this respect as to particular verbs, the idiom itself is a simple one. In passing from one language to another, the construction may have to be altered. The following are the Greek impersonal verbs used in N.T., and nearly all the different forms occur there. Some of these verbs are also found personally. The participle is neuter.

(*a*) δεῖ = it is necessary, it behoves one, one must; imperf. ἐδεῖ, pres. subj. δέῃ, inf. δεῖν, part. δέον. This verb takes the acc. of the person concerned, and the inf. of the verb indicating what it is that must be done.

Example:

δεῖ ὑμᾶς γεννηθῆναι ἄνωθεν (John 3. 7)
= ye must be born again *or* from above

(*b*) δοκεῖ = it seems (fr. δοκέω = I think; cognate with δόξα, the original meaning of which was 'an opinion'); imperf. ἐδόκει, aor. ind. ἔδοξε, pres. part. δοκοῦν. This verb takes the dat. of the person and the inf. of the verb. It often carries with it the idea of approval.

Example:

ἔδοξεν τῷ πνεύματι τῷ ἁγίῳ καὶ ἡμῖν (Acts 15. 28)
= it seemed good to the Holy Spirit and to us

(*c*) ἔξεστι = it is lawful: pres. part. ἔξον. This verb also takes dat. and inf.

Example:

εἰ ἔξεστι τοῖς σάββασιν θεραπεύειν; (Mat. 12. 10)
= is it lawful to heal on the sabbath days?

(*d*) μέλει = it matters, it concerns, it is a care; imperf. ἔμελε. This verb takes the dat. of the person.

Example:

μή σοι μελέτω (I Cor. 7. 21)
= let it not be a care to thee

(*e*) χρή = it is expedient, fitting, congruous. Takes the inf. of the verb.

Example (only one in N.T.):

οὐ χρὴ ταῦτα οὕτω γίνεσθαι (James 3. 10)
= it is not fitting that these things are so

(*f*) πρέπει = it is becoming *or* fitting; imperf. ἔπρεπε, pres. part. πρέπον. Takes the dat. of the person or thing.

Example:

οὕτω γὰρ πρέπον ἐστὶν ἡμῖν πληρῶσαι πᾶσαν δικαιοσύνην
(Mat. 3. 15)
= for so it is becoming to us to fulfil all righteousness

211. Rule 18.   *The genitive of the def. art. with the infinitive of the verb indicates design or result.*

Example:

τοῦ γνῶναι αὐτόν (Phil. 3. 10)
= that I may know him

EXERCISE 31

Give English for:

οὕτως ἔδει παθεῖν τὸν χριστόν. τὸν κοπιῶντα γεωργὸν δεῖ
πρῶτον τῶν καρπῶν μεταλαμβάνειν. τί με δεῖ ποιεῖν ἵνα
σωθῶ; οὐ μέλει τῷ μισθωτῷ περὶ τῶν προβάτων. οὐδὲν
τούτων τῷ Γαλλίωνι ἔμελεν. ἔξεστι τοῖς σάββασι καλῶς
ποιεῖν. ἔλεγεν γὰρ ὁ Ἰωάννης τῷ Ἡρώδῃ ὅτι οὐκ ἔξεστίν σοι
ἔχειν τὴν γυναῖκα τοῦ ἀδελφοῦ σου. τί ὑμῖν δοκεῖ περὶ τοῦ
χριστοῦ; τί σοι δοκεῖ, Σίμων; πρέπον ἐστὶν γυναῖκα
ἀκατακάλυπτον τῷ Θεῷ προσεύχεσθαι; τοιοῦτος γὰρ ἡμῖν
ἔπρεπεν ἀρχιερεύς, ὅσιος, ἄκακος, ἀμίαντος. οἱ ἀπεσταλμένοι
ἦσαν ἐκ τῶν Φαρισαίων. πάλιν ἀπέστειλεν ἄλλους δούλους.

SENTENCES—III. COMPLEX

212. (See paras. 43–45.)   A sentence containing one main predication and one or more subordinate predications is called 'complex'.

Example:

εἰ κεκοίμηται σωθήσεται (John 11. 12)
= if he is asleep he will be healed

Here, 'will be healed' is the main predicate, the pronoun

subject being included in the verb form in the Greek; while 'he is asleep' is subordinate to this, being introduced by 'if'.

OBJECTS

213. A transitive verb takes an object, which may be either direct (acc.) or indirect (gen., dat.). Most such verbs take a direct object.

Example:

> ὁ ἐμὲ μισῶν καὶ τὸν πατέρα μου μισεῖ (John 15. 23)
> = he who hates me hates my Father also

The usages of various languages vary, and in Greek it is necessary to bear in mind that some verbs take the gen. case after them and some the dat.; see paras. 200 and 214.

A verb may have both a direct and an indirect object.

Example:

> ὅσοι ἔλαβον αὐτόν, ἔδωκεν αὐτοῖς ἐξουσίαν τέκνα Θεοῦ
> γενέσθαι, τοῖς πιστεύουσιν εἰς τὸ ὄνομα αὐτοῦ (John
> 1. 12)
> = as many as received him, to them he gave the privilege
> to become God's children—to those [that is] who
> believe in his name

Or two direct objects in apposition.

Example:

> ψεύστην ποιοῦμεν αὐτόν (I John 1. 10)
> = we make him a liar

214. Rule 19. *Adjectives and verbs of filling and of remembering and forgetting take the genitive case* (cp. English 'to be full of', 'to be mindful of', something, respectively).

EXERCISE 32

Give English for:

οἱ δοῦλοι, ὑπακούετε τοῖς κατὰ σάρκα κυρίοις μετὰ φόβου
καὶ τρόμου. οὐ πάντες ὑπήκουσαν τῷ εὐαγγελίῳ. ἐσεβάσ-
θησαν καὶ ἐλάτρευσαν τῇ κτίσει παρὰ τὸν κτίσαντα, ὅς ἐστιν
εὐλογητὸς εἰς τοὺς αἰῶνας. γεμίσατε τὰς ὑδρίας ὕδατος.
ἐπιστραφεὶς ὁ Πέτρος βλέπει τὸν μαθητὴν ὃν ἠγάπα ὁ Ἰησοῦς
ἀκολουθοῦντα, ὃς καὶ ἀνέπεσεν ἐν τῷ δείπνῳ ἐπὶ τὸ στῆθος
αὐτοῦ. μνημόνευε Ἰησοῦ Χριστοῦ.

INTENTIONAL CLAUSES

215. Intentional clauses are those which express purpose or
design; they are introduced by the particle ἵνα (to the end that,
in order that), with emphasis on the *result*, or ὅπως (in such
manner that), with emphasis on the *method*.   These respective
meanings are an attempt to bring out the distinction between
the Greek particles, but should not be taken too rigidly.

Examples:

  ἤδη ὁ θερίζων μισθὸν λαμβάνει καὶ συνάγει καρπὸν εἰς
  ζωὴν αἰώνιον, ἵνα ὁ σπείρων ὁμοῦ χαίρῃ καὶ ὁ θερίζων
  (John 4. 36)
= now he who reaps receives wages and gathers fruit unto
  life eternal, that he who sows and he who reaps may
  rejoice together
  οἱ ὑποκριταὶ ... ἀφανίζουσιν τὰ πρόσωπα αὐτῶν ὅπως
  φανῶσιν τοῖς ἀνθρώποις νηστεύοντες (Mat. 6. 16)
= the hypocrites disfigure their faces so that they may
  appear to men fasting

With regard to ἵνα, commonly translated simply 'that', this
must be carefully distinguished from the conj. ὅτι (that; cp.
para. 205).   Nevertheless, in some passages in N.T. ἵνα is
used where ὅτι might have been expected, as a mere conjunc-

tion; this is notably so in the writings of John (see, *e.g.*, John 17. 3, 6. 29, 15. 12). The reason for this usage is that in N.T. times ἵνα was losing—and had largely lost—its classical intentional force. Yet the equivalence of ἵνα and ὅτι is not to be assumed without adequate reason.

The negative particle appropriate to intentional clauses is of course not the categorical οὐ, denying as a matter of *fact*, but the hypothetical μή, which denies as a matter of *thought*. ἵνα μή = that not = lest; but μή may be elliptical for ἵνα μή or ὅπως μή after verbs of fear, caution, or anxiety, with the meaning 'lest'.

Example:
> σκόπει οὖν μὴ τὸ φῶς τὸ ἐν σοὶ σκότος ἐστίν (Luke 11. 35)
> = consider therefore lest the light that is in thee be darkness

The mood for the verb in an intentional clause is normally the subjunctive, with its general signification of possibility and supposition. However, ἵνα (but not ὅπως) may be found with the fut. ind. The instances of this construction are few, and most of them are contested readings.

In three passages, moreover (I Cor. 4. 6, Gal. 4. 17, Col. 4. 17), the ind. pres. seems to be used in an intentional clause; but in all these the verb is of the A 2 class, ending in όω, and it is better to suppose them to be instances of irregularly formed subjunctive than wrong syntax.

'FINAL' AND 'CONSECUTIVE' CLAUSES

216. A good deal of discussion has taken place on the question whether ἵνα ever means merely 'so that', expressing *event* without any reference to *purpose*. The former presumed use is called the 'ecbatic', or eventual, the latter the 'telic', or final. The telic significance is now felt to be usual if not invariable. This is one of the finer points of N.T. exegesis, and cannot be gone into it fully here. Particular passages are discussed by commentators.

EXERCISE 33

Give English for:

ἐρωτῶ σε, κυρία, οὐχ ὡς ἐντολὴν γράφων σοι καινὴν ἀλλὰ ἣ εἴχαμεν ἀπ' ἀρχῆς, ἵνα ἀγαπῶμεν ἀλλήλους. ταῦτα μελέτα, ἐν τούτοις ἴσθι, ἵνα σου ἡ προκοπὴ φανερὰ ᾖ πᾶσιν. παρεκάλουν αὐτὸν ἵνα μόνον ἅψωνται τοῦ κρασπέδου τοῦ ἱματίου αὐτοῦ. ὁ Ἰησοῦς ἐξέβαλεν τὰ πνεύματα λόγῳ, καὶ πάντας τοὺς κακῶς ἔχοντας ἐθεράπευσεν. ὅπως πληρωθῇ τὸ ῥηθὲν διὰ τοῦ προφήτου. δεήθητε οὖν τοῦ κυρίου τοῦ θερισμοῦ ὅπως ἐκβάλῃ ἐργάτας εἰς τὸν θερισμὸν αὐτοῦ. τότε πορευθέντες οἱ Φαρισαῖοι συμβούλιον ἔλαβον ὅπως αὐτὸν παγιδεύσωσιν ἐν λόγῳ. εἰς ὃ καὶ προσευχόμεθα πάντοτε περὶ ὑμῶν, ἵνα ὑμᾶς ἀξιώσῃ τῆς κλήσεως ὁ Θεὸς ἡμῶν καὶ πληρώσῃ πᾶσαν εὐδοκίαν ἀγαθωσύνης, ὅπως ἐνδοξασθῇ τὸ ὄνομα τοῦ κυρίου ἡμῶν Ἰησοῦ ἐν ὑμῖν.

THE SECOND CONJUGATION

217. We come now to the comparatively small number of verbs of the 2nd or μι conj. It was remarked in para. 113 that this is really the older of the two conjugations. The other and later mode of inflecting the verb, however, gradually tended to displace this, and when the Christian era began the transition from one to the other was in progress; indeed, there are some verbs in N.T. which have alternative inflections—i.e., they are sometimes conjugated as though belonging to the ω and at others to the μι conj. In modern Greek the process is all but complete: with one exception (εἰμί), all the μι verbs have become ω verbs.

In N.T. there are about three dozen μι verbs.

If it was important in the 1st conj. to recognize the stem as distinct from the termination, etc., it is doubly so here; in fact, it is impossible to deal intelligently with μι verbs unless this be done.

The first thing to be noted about them is this:

> *With occasional exceptions, their formation and terminations differ from the 1st conj. only in the pres., imperf., and (where found) 2nd aor. tenses in all moods.*

In all the other tenses they are conjugated exactly as the verbs of the ω conj. already learnt; but this, of course, cannot be done unless and until the true stem is recognized. It should be noted that the rule still holds good that the imperf. has the same stem as the pres., whatever that is.

218. Verbs of the 2nd conj. fall into two main classes:

(a) The first exhibits the stem, lengthened in the act. ind. sing., and generally with an ι reduplication.

(b) The second inserts *ννν* or *νν* (after a vowel or consonant respectively) between stem and termination. These verbs have no second aorists.

Before any verb is set out at length, one example of each of these two classes will show what is involved:

(a) Stem—δο. Pres. ind. act. sing., δί-δω-μι (I give)—the lexical form, corresponding to ——ω of the 1st conj. (See para. 220.)

(b) Stem—δεικ. Pres. ind. act. sing., δείκ-νυ-μι (I show). (See para. 225.)

In class (a) the stem is preceded by a kind of reduplication, which must not be confused with the normal ε reduplication characteristic of the perfect tenses; instances of this ι reduplication have been seen in the 1st conj.—γίνομαι (para. 194), γινώσκω (para. 204), etc. The stem vowel is then lengthened, but only in the sing.; then the personal ending follows.

In class (*b*) the stem remains unaltered, followed by the element νυ or ννυ, and then the personal ending. In this class especially are found some verbs oscillating between the two conjugations—*e.g.* δείκνυμι, δεικνύω.

Now, in all tenses except those above mentioned it can be taken as a general rule that the mode of inflection of an ω verb applies to a μι verb as well. Thus, taking two other verbs as typical—

(*a*) τίθημι (I place); stem—θε. Fut. ind. θήσω (stem vowel lengthened as for ε verbs of 1st conj.—class A 2); pres.-perf. τέθεικα; past-perf. (ἐ)τεθείκειν; 1st aor. ind. is, however, ἔθηκα—κ instead of σ (δίδωμι and ἵημι are the only other two verbs to do this).

(*b*) ζώννυμι (I gird); stem—ζο. Fut. ind. ζώσω; pres.-perf. ἔζωκα.

The same general principles apply in both conjugations: the augment for past tenses in the indicative mood, and the reduplication in the perfect tenses in all moods, as seen above. Of course, the corresponding tenses in the other moods are formed analogously.

Full conjugations of some μι verbs in so far as they differ in their inflection from the 1st conj. will now be given, these 2nd conj. verbs not being so easy to follow from their terminations alone.

EXERCISE 34

Give English for:

τὴν ψυχήν μου τίθημι ὑπὲρ τῶν προβάτων. ἀναγαγὼν τὸν Ἰησοῦν, ὁ διάβολος ἔδειξεν αὐτῷ πάσας τὰς βασιλείας τῆς οἰκουμένης ἐν στιγμῇ χρόνου. σοὶ δώσω τὴν ἐξουσίαν ταύτην ἅπασαν καὶ τὴν δόξαν αὐτῶν, ὅτι ἐμοὶ παραδέδοται καὶ ᾧ ἂν θέλω δίδωμι αὐτήν. σεαυτὸν δεῖξον τῷ ἱερεῖ. ὑμῖν δείξει ἀνάγαιον. δείξατέ μοι δηνάριον. δείξω σοι ἃ δεῖ γενέσθαι

μετὰ ταῦτα. αἰτεῖτε, καὶ δοθήσεται ὑμῖν. ἡ σελήνη οὐ
δώσει τὸ φέγγος αὐτῆς. ὁ νόμος διὰ Μωυσέως ἐδόθη, ἡ
χάρις καὶ ἡ ἀλήθεια διὰ Ἰησοῦ Χριστοῦ ἐγένετο. ὥστε,
ἀγαπητοί μου, μετὰ φόβου καὶ τρόμου τὴν ἑαυτῶν σωτηρίαν
κατεργάζεσθε.

CONDITIONAL SENTENCES

219. A 'conditional sentence' really consists of two sentences—
one expressing the condition, and the other that which depends
on the condition. We discard the terms 'protasis' and
'apodosis', formerly used by grammarians, and follow rather
the recommendation of the Joint Committee on Grammatical
Terminology, and refer to these two sentences by the simple
English terms 'if' and 'then' clauses respectively. The purport
of such terms is obvious.

There are four kinds of condition, supposition, or hypo-
thesis:

1. The supposition of a fact—in past, present, or future
   time.
2. The supposition of a possibility, where experience will
   decide whether the thing is really so or not.
3. The supposition of an uncertainty—a condition merely
   supposed in thought.
4. The supposition of something unfulfilled—the belief
   being entertained that the condition is not a fact.

We give these now in their English forms, and shall then
proceed to give some Greek sentences, illustrating each kind,
as they occur in N.T. Thus:

'If' clause—	'Then' clause—
1. If you command,	I obey.
2. If you command,	I shall obey.
3. If you should command,	I will obey.
4. If you had commanded,	I should have ...

The English phrasing may vary, but the distinction between these four statements is clear.

CONJUGATION OF δίδωμι

220. Here is the conjugation of this verb in full in the three tenses which differ from the 1st conj. All the other tenses are formed regularly, from the stem δο, after the model of the 1st conj.: fut. ind. δώσω, δώσομαι, δοθήσομαι; pres.-perf. δέδωκα, δέδομαι; past-perf. (ἐ)δεδώκειν, (ἐ)δέδομην; 1st aor. act. ἔδωκα, pass. ἐδόθην (this verb has no 2nd aor. pass.); and analogously in other moods.

For economy of space, the three voices are given together: top line, act., with mid.-pass. underneath except as otherwise indicated. Some forms do not exist.

INDICATIVE MOOD

Present:

δίδωμι	-δως	-δωσι	-δομεν	-δοτε	-δόασι
-δομαι	-δοσαι	-δοται	-δόμεθα	-δοσθε	-δονται

Imperfect (with augment—see para. 115 (d))*:

ἐδίδων	-δως	-δω	-δομεν	-δοτε	-δοσαν
-δόμην	-δοσο†	-δοτο	-δόμεθα	-δοσθε	-δοντο

Second Aorist (with augment):

		ἔδομεν	ἔδοτε	ἔδοσαν

ἐδόμην,‡ etc., as for the imperf., but without the ι reduplication; see para. 188 for the formation of 2nd aor. tenses generally.

SUBJUNCTIVE MOOD

Present:

διδῶ	-δῶς	-δῷ	-δῶμεν	-δῶτε	-δῶσι
-δῶμαι	-δῷ	-δῶται	-δώμεθα	-δῶσθε	-δῶνται

* See para. 217 *ad fin.*
† The termination οσο may or may not be found contracted to ου; σ is often dropped between two short vowels, with resulting contraction.
‡ Middle voice only; see above.

Second Aorist (without augment—see para. 115 (*j*)): δῶ, etc., like the pres. act., without reduplication. δῶμαι,‡ etc., like the pres. mid., without reduplication.

OPTATIVE MOOD

Present:

διδοίην	-δοίης	-δοίη	-δοῖμεν	-δοῖτε	-δοῖεν
-δοίμην	-δοῖο	-δοῖτο	-δοίμεθα	-δοῖσθε	-δοῖντο

Second Aorist:

δοίην	δοίης	δοίη	δοίημεν	δοίητε	δοῖεν

δοίμην,‡ etc., like the pres. mid., without reduplication.

IMPERATIVE MOOD

Present:

δίδου	διδότω	δίδοτε	διδότωσαν
δίδοσο†	διδόσθω	δίδοσθε	διδόσθωσαν

Second Aorist:

δός	δότω	δότε	δότωσαν
δοῦ†‡	δόσθω	δόσθε	δόσθωσαν

THE INFINITIVE

Present: act. διδόναι; mid.-pass. δίδοσθαι

Second Aorist: act. δοῦναι; mid. δόσθαι‡

THE PARTICIPLES

Present: act. διδούς, διδοῦσα, διδόν; mid.-pass. διδόμενος, διδομένη, διδόμενον

Second Aorist: act. δούς, δοῦσα, δόν; mid. δόμενος,‡ δομένη, δόμενον

* See footnote * on previous page.
† See footnote † on previous page.
‡ See footnote ‡ on previous page.

EXERCISE 35

Give English for:

τῷ αἰτοῦντί σε δίδου. τὸν ἄρτον ἡμῶν τὸν ἐπιούσιον δὸς
ἡμῖν σήμερον. μὴ δῶτε τὸ ἅγιον τοῖς κυσίν. ὑμῖν δέδοται
γνῶναι τὰ μυστήρια τῆς βασιλείας τοῦ Θεοῦ. οἱ ὄχλοι
ἐφοβήθησαν καὶ ἐδόξασαν τὸν Θεὸν τὸν δόντα ἐξουσίαν
τοιαύτην τοῖς ἀνθρώποις. ἔξεστι δοῦναι κῆνσον Καίσαρι ἢ οὔ;
προσκαλεσάμενος τοὺς δώδεκα μαθητὰς αὐτοῦ ἔδωκεν αὐτοῖς
ἐξουσίαν πνευμάτων ἀκαθάρτων ὥστε ἐκβάλλειν αὐτὰ καὶ
θεραπεύειν πᾶσαν νόσον καὶ πᾶσαν μαλακίαν. τὸν ἄρτον ἡμῶν
τὸν ἐπιούσιον δίδου ἡμῖν τὸ καθ᾽ ἡμέραν. δῶμεν τὴν δόξαν
αὐτῷ.

CONDITIONAL SENTENCES

1. *The Supposition of a Fact*

221. Here the conditional particle εἰ (if; not to be confused with
εἶ, thou art) is used, with the ind. mood, in the 'if' clause,
assuming the fact, and either the ind. or the imperat. (or subj.
with οὐ μή if a prohibition) in the 'then' clause; that is to say,
such-and-such a result follows, or will follow, or a course of
action is indicated, the fact being as stated.

Examples:

εἰ νεκροὶ οὐκ ἐγείρονται, οὐδὲ Χριστὸς ἐγήγερται (I Cor.
15. 16)

= if dead persons are not raised, neither has Christ been
raised

εἰ θέλεις εἰς τὴν ζωὴν εἰσελθεῖν, τήρει τὰς ἐντολάς (Mat.
19. 16)

= if thou wishest to enter into life, keep the commandments

CONJUGATION OF τίθημι

222. We shall give in full two other verbs in class (a) (see para.
218) of the 2nd conj.; this, because the conjugation of these μι

verbs is not so easy to follow, by the terminations alone, as are the ω verbs.

The verb given in para. 220 had δο as its stem. The one now given has an ε stem—θε. The ε is lengthened to η just as ο is to ω; but the reduplication takes the form of τι—i.e., the sharp τ corresponding to the aspirate θ is used (see table, para. 10), as in the perfects of other verbs (e.g., πεφόνευκα). The result is τίθημι = I put, place; the τι appearing in all the pres. and imperf. tenses.

The top line under each tense gives the endings for the active voice, and those underneath the mid. and pass., unless otherwise indicated.

INDICATIVE MOOD

Present:

τίθημι	-θης	-θησι	-θεμεν	-θετε	-θέασι
-θεμαι	-θεσαι*	-θεται	-θέμεθα	-θεσθε	-θενται

Imperfect (with augment—see para. 115 (d)):

ἐτίθην	-θης	-θη	-θεμεν	-θετε	-θεσαν
-θέμην	-θεσο†	-θετο	-θέμεθα	-θεσθε	-θεντο

Second Aorist (with augment):

ἔθεμεν	ἔθετε	ἔθεσαν

ἐθέμην,‡ etc., as for the imperf., but without the ι reduplication.

---

* Or τίθη.

† The termination εσο may or may not be found contracted to ου.

‡ Mid. only. This verb, like δίδωμι, has no 2nd aor. pass., but a regularly formed 1st aor. pass. as of the 1st conj.—ἐτέθην, etc. (the θ of the stem becomes τ on account of the termination beginning with θ; this is to avoid two θ's coming in contiguous syllables—cp. ἐτύθη in 1 Cor. v. 8. from θύω, and see para. 161 *ad fin.*).

Present:

τιθῶ	-θῃς	-θῇ	-θῶμεν	-θῆτε	-θῶσι
-θῶμαι	-θῇ	-θῆται	-θώμεθα	-θῆσθε	-θῶνται

Second Aorist (without augment—see para. 115 (*j*)): θῶ, etc., like the pres. act., without reduplication. θῶμαι,† etc., like the pres. mid., without reduplication.

OPTATIVE MOOD

Present:

τιθείην	-θείης	-θείη	-θεῖμεν	-θεῖτε	-θεῖεν
-θείμην	-θεῖο	-θεῖτο	-θείμεθα	-θεῖσθε	-θεῖντο

Second Aorist:

θείην	θείης	θείη	θείημεν	θείητε	θεῖεν

θείμην,† etc., like the pres. mid., without reduplication.

IMPERATIVE MOOD

Present:

τίθει	τιθέτω		τίθετε	τιθέτωσαν
τίθεσο*	τιθέσθω		τίθεσθε	τιθέσθωσαν

Second Aorist:

θές	θέτω		θέτε	θέτωσαν
θοῦ*†	θέσθω		θέσθε	θέσθωσαν

THE INFINITIVE

Present: act. τιθέναι, mid.-pass. τίθεσθαι
Second Aorist: act. θεῖναι, mid. θέσθαι†

THE PARTICIPLES

Present: act. τιθείς, τιθεῖσα, τιθέν; mid.-pass. τιθέμενος, τιθεμένη, τιθέμενον

* See footnote † on previous page.
† See footnote ‡ on previous page.

Second Aorist: act. θείς, θεῖσα, θέν; mid. θέμενος,* θεμένη, θέμενον

Other tenses: fut. ind. θήσω, θήσομαι, τεθήσομαι; and see para. 218, the mid.-pass. of the perfects being formed analogously.

EXERCISE 36

Give English for:

λέγει ὁ διάβολος τῷ Ἰησοῦ, Εἰ υἱὸς εἶ τοῦ Θεοῦ, βάλε σεαυτὸν κάτω. εἰ ἑκὼν τοῦτο πράσσω, μισθὸν ἔχω· εἰ δὲ ἄκων, οἰκονομίαν πεπίστευμαι. εἰ οὖν συνηγέρθητε τῷ Χριστῷ, τὰ ἄνω ζητεῖτε. εἰ οὐκ ἐγκρατεύονται, γαμησάτωσαν. ἐκεῖ ἔθηκαν τὸ τοῦ Ἰησοῦ σῶμα. ἔθεντο οἱ ἀκούσαντες τὰ ῥήματα ταῦτα ἐν τῇ καρδίᾳ αὐτῶν. ποῦ τεθείκατε αὐτόν; Θεὸς ἦν ἐν Χριστῷ τὸν κόσμον καταλλάσσων ἑαυτῷ, μὴ λογιζόμενος αὐτοῖς τὰ παραπτώματα αὐτῶν, καὶ θέμενος ἐν ἡμῖν τὸν λόγον τῆς καταλλαγῆς. τί ἔθου ἐν τῇ καρδίᾳ σου τὸ πρᾶγμα τοῦτο; πατέρα πολλῶν ἐθνῶν τέθεικά σε. θεὶς τὰ γόνατα ὁ Ἰησοῦς προσηύχετο λέγων, Πάτερ, εἰ βούλει παρένεγκε (bear away) τοῦτο τὸ ποτήριον ἀπ' ἐμοῦ· πλὴν μὴ τὸ θέλημά μου ἀλλὰ τὸ σὸν γινέσθω.

CONJUGATION OF ἵστημι

223. We now give a verb, belonging to class *a* of the 2nd conj., with an α stem. This verb too is of fairly frequent occurrence in N.T., both in its simple form and compounded with a preposition.

The stem is στα (cp. στάσις = standing, Heb. 9. 8); the reduplication here, however, takes the form of an aspirated ι, while the α is lengthened to η; hence ἵστημι = I stand *or* place.

* See footnote ‡ on page 133.

INDICATIVE MOOD

Present:

ἵστημι	-στης	-στησι	-σταμεν	-στατε	-στασι
ἵσταμαι	-στασαι	-σταται	-στάμεθα	-στασθε	-στανται

Imperfect*:

ἵστην	-στης	-στη	-σταμεν	-στατε	-στασαν
ἱστάμην	-στασο	-στατο	-στάμεθα	-στασθε	-σταντο

Second Aorist (with augment)†:

ἔστην	ἔστης	ἔστη	ἔστημεν	ἔστητε	ἔστησαν

SUBJUNCTIVE MOOD

Present:

ἱστῶ	-στῇς	-στῇ	-στῶμεν	-στῆτε	-στῶσι
ἱστῶμαι	-στῃ	-στηται	-στώμεθα	-στῆσθε	-στῶνται

Second Aorist (without augment—see para. 115 (*j*))†: στῶ, etc., like the pres. act., without reduplication.

OPTATIVE MOOD

Present:

ἱσταίην	-σταίης	-σταίη	-σταῖμεν	-σταῖτε	-σταῖεν
ἱσταίμην	-σταῖο	-σταῖτο	-σταίμεθα	-σταῖσθε	-σταῖντο

Second Aorist†:

σταίην	σταίης	σταίη	σταίημεν	σταίητε	σταῖεν

IMPERATIVE MOOD

Present:

ἵστη	ἱστάτω	ἵστατε	ἱστάτωσαν
ἵστασο ‡	ἱστάσθω	ἵστασθε	ἱστάσθωσαν

Second Aorist†:

στῆθι§	στήτω	στῆτε	στήτωσαν

---

* No augment is possible in the imperf., on account of the unusual form of the reduplication.

† Active voice only. This verb has no 2nd aor. mid. or pass., but forms both these voices in the 1st aor. after the model of the 1st conj.—ἐστησάμην, ἐστάθην, respectively.

‡ Or ἵστω.

§ But στά in compound verbs.

THE INFINITIVE

Present: act. ἵσταναι; mid.-pass. ἵστασθαι

Second Aorist*: στῆναι

THE PARTICIPLES

Present: act. ἱστάς, ἱστᾶσα, ἱστάν; mid.-pass. ἱστάμενος, ἱσταμένη, ἱστάμενον.

Second Aorist*: στάς, στᾶσα, στάν.

The remaining tenses are, as in all μι verbs (see para. 217), regularly formed: fut. ind. στήσω, στήσομαι, σταθήσομαι, 1st aor. act. (see note * above for mid. and pass.) ἔστησα, pres.-perf. ἕστηκα, ἕσταμαι (note the aspirate, again serving for the reduplication), past-perf. εἱστήκειν, ἑστάμην. So in the other moods, etc. (and, of course, in all compounds), except that there is a syncopated form of some of the perfs. in frequent use—*e.g.* ἕσταμεν for ἑστήκαμεν.

NOTE. The meaning of this verb requires careful attention. It is *transitive* in pres., imperf., fut., and 1st aor., and then means 'set up', 'place', etc.; but it is *intransitive* (*i.e.*, it has no object) in 2nd aor. and perfs., with the meaning 'stand'.

CONDITIONAL SENTENCES

2. *The Supposition of a Possibility*

224. Objective possibility, or uncertainty with the prospect of decision, is expressed by ἐάν (*i.e.*, εἰ ἄν), with the subj. in the 'if' clause and the ind. (or aor. subj. with οὐ μή) or imperat. in the 'then' clause. Very rarely, εἰ only is used. After ἄν and its compounds (ὅταν = ὅτε ἄν, whenever; etc.) the subj. is always used in such clauses.

Examples:

ἐάν τις θελῇ τὸ θέλημα αὐτοῦ ποιεῖν, γνώσεται περὶ τῆς διδαχῆς πότερον ἐκ τοῦ θεοῦ ἐστιν ἢ ἐγὼ ἀπ' ἐμαυτοῦ λαλῶ (John 7. 17)

* See footnote † on previous page.

= if anyone is willing to do his will, he shall know concerning the teaching whether it is of God or (whether)
I speak from myself

ἐὰν τὸ ἅλας μωρανθῇ, ἐν τίνι ἁλισθήσεται; (Mat. 5. 13)
= if the salt is corrupted, wherewith shall it be salted?

The condition refers to future time—hence the use of the
fut. ind. or its equivalent, in a negative statement, the aor.
subj. with οὐ μή.

EXERCISE 37

Give English for:

ἐάν τις τὸν λόγον μου τηρήσῃ, οὐ μὴ γεύσεται θανάτου εἰς
τὸν αἰῶνα. ἐάν τις διψᾷ, ἐρχέσθω πρός με καὶ πινέτω. ἐὰν ἡ
ἀκροβυστία τὰ δικαιώματα τοῦ νόμου φυλάσσῃ, οὐχ ἡ ἀκροβυστία αὐτοῦ εἰς περιτομὴν λογισθήσεται; σωθήσεται διὰ τῆς
τεκνογονίας, ἐὰν μείνωσιν ἐν πίστει καὶ ἀγάπῃ καὶ ἁγιασμῷ
μετὰ σωφροσύνης. ἐὰν ᾖ ἡ οἰκία ἀξία, ἐλθάτω ἡ εἰρήνη ὑμῶν
ἐπ' αὐτήν. προσκαλεσάμενος παιδίον ἔστησεν ὁ Ἰησοῦς αὐτὸ
ἐν μέσῳ αὐτῶν. στήσει τὰ μὲν πρόβατα ἐκ δεξιῶν αὐτοῦ τὰ δὲ
ἐρίφια ἐξ εὐωνύμων. πῶς σταθήσεται ἡ βασιλεία αὐτοῦ;

SECOND CONJUGATION—CLASS B

225. Except for the defective and a few other verbs calling for
special notice, all that now remains of the Greek verb system
is the second class (*b*) of verbs in μι (cp. paras. 217, 218). As
there remarked, these verbs have no 2nd aor., so that only the
pres. and imperf. have to be considered, all the other tenses
being formed from the stem as though belonging to the 1st
conj.

Some of the verbs belonging to this class have, in pres. and
imperf., an alternative formation as if they belonged to the
1st conj. here also; *e.g.*, from the stem δεικ we find δεικνύω as
well as δείκνυμι, and as such a form corresponds to Class A 1

(uncontracted) no difficulty in conjugation can occur. But in so far as they are conjugated according to the 2nd conj., the terminations are exactly as those given for class *a* (see paras. 220, 222, and 223), which it is therefore not necessary to repeat.

This alternation between the two ways of conjugating is of historical interest, as marking a stage in the passing of the older conjugation to the newer—to which all verbs in modern Greek, with one exception (εἰμί), conform.

The stem may be consonantal (δεικ) or vowel (σβε). With this as a starting-point, the element νυ or ννυ is added respectively, and then the ending follows this. These verbs are of rare occurrence, and should not occasion great difficulty.

CONDITIONAL SENTENCES

3. *The Supposition of Uncertainty*

226. The optative mood in a conditional clause expresses entire uncertainty—a supposed case (subjective possibility, cp. para. 224). The particle εἰ is always used here. This construction is not very common in N.T.

Example:

> οὓς ἔδει ἐπὶ σοῦ παρεῖναι καὶ κατηγορεῖν, εἰ τι ἔχοιεν πρός με (Acts 24. 19)
>
> = who ought to have been here, and to make accusation, if they had [in their own belief—Moulton] anything against me

This usage occurs parenthetically in the phrase εἰ τύχοι (2nd aor. opt. of τυγχάνω, fall out, happen) = if it should chance (1 Cor. 14. 10, 15. 37); and εἰ θέλοι τὸ θέλημα τοῦ Θεοῦ = if the will of God should will (it) (1 Pet. 3. 17).

EXERCISE 38

Give English for:

ἀλλὰ καὶ ἐὰν ἡμεῖς ἢ ἄγγελος ἐξ οὐρανοῦ εὐαγγελίσηται

ὑμῖν παρ' ὃ εὐαγγελισάμεθα ὑμῖν, ἀνάθεμα ἔστω. πάλιν λέγω,
εἴ τις ὑμᾶς εὐαγγελίζεται παρ' ὃ παρελάβετε, ἀνάθεμα ἔστω.
μὴ ἀντιστῆναι τῷ πονηρῷ. τὸ πνεῦμα μὴ σβέννυτε. ἀπόδοτε
τὰ Καίσαρος Καίσαρι καὶ τὰ τοῦ Θεοῦ τῷ Θεῷ. αἱ λαμπάδες
ἡμῶν σβέννυνται. ἀποδώσει ἑκάστῳ κατὰ τὰ ἔργα αὐτοῦ.
ἰδοὺ, ἕστηκα ἐπὶ τὴν θύραν καὶ κρούω. γνόντες τὴν χάριν τὴν
δοθεῖσάν μοι, Ἰάκωβος καὶ Κηφᾶς καὶ Ἰωάννης δεξιὰς ἔδωκαν
ἐμοὶ καὶ Βαρνάβᾳ κοινωνίας. σὺ τῇ πίστει ἕστηκας. λίνον
τυφόμενον οὐ σβέσει. ζῶσαι.

SECOND CONJUGATION
Deponents

As in the 1st conj. (see para. 172), so in the 2nd there are
verbs which have no active form, but are conjugated in the
middle and/or passive with an active meaning. Five of these
call for attention, as occurring in the N.T. The first of them,
in the order now given, is fairly common.

227. δύναμαι (stem—δυνα), I can, am able. Pres. ind. μαι,
-σαι (or δύνῃ), -ται, etc.; imperf. ἐδυνάμην or ἠδυνάμην
(double augment); aor. ἐδυνήθην, ἠδυνήθην, or ἠδυνάσθην; fut.
δυνήσομαι; pres. subj. δύνωμαι; opt. δυναίμην; inf. δύνασθαι;
part. δυνάμενος. There is an adjective formed from this verb
—δυνατός, ή, όν, having power; in Luke 1. 49 ὁ δυνατός
(= the Mighty One) is a periphrasis for God, in accordance
with Jewish custom. This verb takes a dependent infinitive
to complete its sense (see para. 138 (iii)).

Example:
    διὰ τί ἡμεῖς οὐκ ἠδυνήθημεν ἐκβαλεῖν αὐτό; (Mat. 17. 19)
    = why were we not able to expel it?

228. ἐπίσταμαι (stem—στα, with ἐπί prefixed, but without ἰ),
I know, am sure; *lit.* I take my stand on.
    Only in pres. mid. in the N.T., and pres. part. ἐπιστάμενος.

229. κρέμαμαι (stem—κρεμα), I hang.

Pres. ind., 3rd pers. sing. κρέμαται, pl. -νται; aor. ἐκρεμάσθην; aor. subj. κρεμασθῶ; pres. part. κρεμάμενος; aor. part. κρεμασθείς.

230. ἧμαι (stem—ἐ), I am seated; a perf. mid. or pass., as from ἕω, I set or seat, ἕομαι, I seat myself, hence ἧμαι, I have seated myself, and so am now sitting. In N.T. found only in composition with κατά, down.

Pres. ind., κάθημαι (2nd pers. sing. κάθῃ, for κάθησαι); imperf. ἐκαθήμην, properly a past-perf.; imperat. κάθου, for κάθησο; inf. καθῆσθαι; part. καθήμενος (as in the Apocalypse, ὁ καθήμενος = the one sitting, the sitter, in reference to the throne).

231. κεῖμαι (stem—κε), I lie down; also properly a perf.—I have laid myself, or have been laid, down. Imperf. ἐκείμην; inf. κεῖσθαι; part. κείμενος.

CONDITIONAL SENTENCES
4. *The Supposition of Something Unfulfilled*

232. When the condition is spoken of as unfulfilled, the ind. mood is used in both clauses, with the particle εἰ in the 'if' clause and ἄν in the 'then' clause. (This use of ἄν must be distinguished from that in which it governs the subj.) But the following distinction is to be noted.

(*a*) The imperf. in the 'then' clause with ἄν points to *present* time—'if this were so now' (which it is not).

Example:

εἰ ὁ Θεὸς πατὴρ ὑμῶν ἦν ἠγαπᾶτε ἂν ἐμέ (John 8. 42)
= if God were your Father ye would love me

(*b*) The aor. with ἄν points to the *past*—'if this had been so then' (which it was not). Sometimes the past-perf. is used more emphatically in the same sense.

Example:

> εἰ γὰρ ἔγνωσαν, οὐκ ἂν τὸν Κύριον τῆς δόξης ἐσταύρωσαν (1 Cor. 2. 8)
> = for if they had known, they would not have crucified the Lord of glory

EXERCISE 39

Give English for:

ἡ ἀξίνη πρὸς τὴν ῥίζαν τῶν δένδρων κεῖται. οὐ δύναται πόλις κρυβῆναι ἐπάνω ὄρους κειμένη. οὐκ ἐπίστασθε τὰ τῆς αὔριον. Κύριε, αὐτοὶ ἐπίστανται ὅτι ἐγὼ ἤμην φυλακίζων καὶ δέρων κατὰ τὰς συναγωγὰς τοὺς πιστεύοντας ἐπὶ σέ. ἐπικατάρατος πᾶς ὁ κρεμάμενος ἐπὶ ξύλον. ἦχος ἐπλήρωσεν ὅλον τὸν οἶκον οὗ ἦσαν καθήμενοι. οὐ δυνάμεθα ἀρνεῖσθαι. εἴ τι δύνῃ, βοήθησον ἡμῖν σπλαγχνισθεὶς ἐφ' ἡμᾶς. ἄγγελος Κυρίου καταβὰς ἐξ οὐρανοῦ ἀπεκύλισε τὸν λίθον καὶ ἐκάθητο ἐπάνω αὐτοῦ.

SECOND CONJUGATION
Special

233. If now we deal with two verbs belonging to the 2nd conj., but calling for special attention, we shall conclude the accidence of the Greek verb except for the defective verbs, and there will be no verb form which cannot be understood in the light of the instruction given.

These two verbs are not unlike the substantive verb εἰμί, and therefore need to be carefully distinguished from it. One is εἶμι, I go (stem—*i*), and the other ἵημι, I send (stem—*ἑ*).

But neither occurs in the N.T. in its simple form—only in composition; for example, respectively,

σύνειμι (σύν + εἶμι), I go with, accompany;
ἀφίημι (ἀπό + ἵημι), I send away, forgive, etc.

The latter most important compound is now given in full (active voice first, middle and passive below), while the few necessary forms of εἶμι, to show the difference between it and the substantive verb, follow in para. 235.

CONJUGATION OF ἀφίημι

234. The stem being ἐ, reduplication produces ἵημι. The preposition ἀπό (from, away from) is prefixed; the o is elided before ἱ, and as this is aspirated the π becomes φ. Hence ἀφίημι.

It has still to be borne in mind that only three tenses need special consideration—pres., imperf., and 2nd aor. (paras. 217, 218). The other tenses can be readily traced by the aid of the schemes of terminations of the 1st conj.—*e.g.* fut. ind. act. ἀφήσω, pres.-perf. ἀφεῖκα, 1st aor. ἄφηκα (cp. δίδωμι and τίθημι).

INDICATIVE MOOD

Present:

ἀφ | ίημι, ίης or εἶς, ίησιν, ίεμεν, ίετε, ἱᾶσιν or ἱοῦσιν
ἀφίε | μαι, σαι, ται   μεθα, σθε, νται

Imperfect (preposition augmented in act.):

ἤφι | ον, ες, ε   plural wanting
ἀφιέ | μην, σο, το   μεθα, σθε, ντο

Second Aorist:

singular wanting   ἀφ | εἶμεν, εἶτε, εἶσαν

*ἀφεί | μην, then as imperf.

* Middle only. There is a 1st aor. pass., formed regularly from the stem ἀφε, with the terminations of the 1st conj.—ἀφέθην, etc.

SUBJUNCTIVE MOOD

Present:

| ἀφί | ω, ῇς, ῇ | ὦμεν, ῆτε, ὦσιν |
| ἀφι | ῶμαι, ῇ, ῆται | ώμεθα, ῆσθε, ωνται |

Second Aorist (without augment—see para. 115 (*j*)):

ἀφ | ῶ, ῇς, ῇ   ὦμεν, ῆτε, ὦσιν

*ἀφ | ῶμαι, then as pres.

OPTATIVE MOOD

Present:

ἀφι | είην, είης, είη   εἶμεν, εἶτε, εἶεν

ἀφι | οίμην or είμην, οἶο or εἶο, οἶτο or εἶτο, etc.

Second Aorist:

ἀφ | είην, then as pres.

*ἀφ | οίμην, then as pres.

IMPERATIVE MOOD

Present:

| ἀφί | ει, έτω | ετε, έτωσαν |
| ἀφί | εσο or ου, έσθω | εσθε, έσθωσαν |

Second Aorist:

ἀφ | ες, έτω   ετε, έτωσαν

*ἄφ | ου, then as pres.

THE INFINITIVE

Present: act. ἀφιέναι; mid.-pass. ἀφίεσθαι.

Second Aorist: ἀφεῖναι; mid. ἀφέσθαι.*

THE PARTICIPLES

Present: act. ἀφι | είς, εῖσα, έν; mid.-pass. έμενος, εμένη, έμενον.

Second Aorist: act. ἀφ |είς, εῖσα, έν; mid. έμενος, εμένη, έμενον.*

*See footnote * on previous page.

The mid.-pass. of the pres.-perf. is ἀφεῖμαι, and of the past-perf. ἀφείμην.

EXERCISE 40

Give English for:

τότε ἀφίησεν αὐτὸν ὁ διάβολος. ἐὰν ἀφῆτε τοῖς ἀνθρώποις τὰ παραπτώματα αὐτῶν, ἀφήσει καὶ ὑμῖν ὁ πατὴρ ὑμῶν ὁ οὐράνιος. ἄφες ἐκεῖ τὸ δῶρόν σου ἔμπροσθεν τοῦ θυσιαστήριον. ἀφῆκεν αὐτὴν ὁ πυρετός. ἐξουσίαν ἔχει ὁ υἱὸς τοῦ ἀνθρώπου ἐπὶ τῆς γῆς ἀφιέναι ἁμαρτίας. ἄφετε συναυξάνεσθαι ἀμφότερα ἕως τοῦ θερισμοῦ. ἀφίεται ὑμῖν ὁ οἶκος ὑμῶν ἔρημος. οὐκ ἤφιε λαλεῖν τὰ δαιμόνια. ἀγάπην σου τὴν πρώτην ἀφῆκας.

FORMS OF εἰμι

235.

Indicative Present:

εἶμι	εἶ	εἶσι	ἴμεν	ἴτε	ἴασι(ν)

Imperfect:

ἤειν	ἤεις	ἤει	ἤειμεν	ἤειτε	ἤεσαν

Imperative Present:

—	ἴθι	ἴτω	—	ἴτε	ἴτωσαν

Subjunctive Present:

ἴω	ἴῃς	ἴῃ	ἴωμεν	ἴητε	ἴωσι(ν)

Optative Present:

ἴοιμι	ἴοις	ἴοι	ἴοιμεν	ἴοιτε	ἴοιεν

Infinitive Present: ἰέναι.

Participle Present: m. ἰών, f. ἰοῦσα, n. ἰόν.

NUMERAL ADJECTIVES

Concluded

236. The cardinal numbers from 'thirteen' to 'nineteen' are formed by the combination of δέκα (para. 92) with the desired unit, after the analogy of 'eleven' and 'twelve', but with καί, and the unit, perhaps, being modified. The ordinals are formed regularly. Thus—

13. τρισκαίδεκα	τρισκαιδέκατος, η, ον
14. τεσσαρεσκαίδεκα	
or δεκατέσσαρες	τεσσαρακαιδέκατος
15. πεντεκαίδεκα or δέκα πέντε	πεντεκαιδέκατος
16. ἑκκαίδεκα	ἑκκαιδέκατος
17. ἑπτακαίδεκα	ἑπτακαιδέκατος
18. ὀκτωκαίδεκα or	
δέκα καὶ ὀκτώ	ὀκτωκαιδέκατος
19. ἐννεακαίδεκα	ἐννεακαιδέκατος

From 'twenty-one' onward this process is repeated, with or without καί. Thus—

20. εἴκοσι(ν)		εἰκοστός, ή, όν
21.	καὶ εἷς (μία, ἕν)	εἰκοστὸς καὶ πρῶτος
22.	καὶ δύο	δεύτερος

So for the remaining tens, -κοντα answering to the English '-ty'. Thus—

30. τριάκοντα	τριακοστός, ή, όν
40. τεσσαράκοντα	τεσσαρακοστός
50. πεντήκοντα	πεντηκοστός
60. ἑξήκοντα	ἑξηκοστός
70. ἑβδομήκοντα	ἑβδομηκοστός
80. ὀγδοήκοντα	ὀγδοηκοστός
90. ἐνενήκοντα	ἐνενηκοστός

The word for 'hundred' is indeclinable—

100. ἑκατόν	ἑκατοστός, ή, όν

but those for the succeeding hundreds are declined as plurals. Thus—

200. διακόσιοι, αι, α	διακοσιοστός, ή, όν

The word for 'thousand', however, is a plural—

1,000. χίλιοι, αι, α   χιλιοστός, ή, όν

(But note that the noun 'thousand' is χιλιάς.)

Then the succeeding thousands follow regularly—

2,000. δισχίλιοι, αι, α   δισχιλιοστός, ή, όν
3,000. τρισχίλιοι   τρισχιλιοστός
4,000. τετρακισχίλιοι   τετρακισχιλιοστός

and so on, as for the hundreds.

The word for 'ten thousand' is μύριοι, αι, α, and the ordinal μυριοστός, ή, όν.

In making up compound numbers, the largest is placed first, and the smaller follow in order, with or without καί. The smaller number is sometimes attached to the larger as one word.

Where the modified noun is unexpressed because understood from the context or otherwise, the numeral is constructed with the appropriate article only.

Example:

ἐὰν γένηταί τινι ἀνθρώπῳ ἑκατὸν πρόβατα καὶ πλανηθῇ ἓν ἐξ αὐτῶν, οὐχὶ ἀφήσει τὰ ἐνενήκοντα ἐννέα ἐπὶ τὰ ὄρη καὶ πορευθεὶς ζητεῖ τὸ πλανώμενον; (Mat. 18. 12)

= if a man should have a hundred sheep, and one of them wander, will he not leave the ninety-nine on the hills and go and seek the wandering one?

EXERCISE 41

Give English for:

ἐν ἔτει πεντεκαιδεκάτῳ τῆς ἡγεμονίας Τιβερίου Καίσαρος. τεσσαράκοντα καὶ ἓξ ἔτεσιν οἰκοδομήθη ὁ ναὸς οὗτος. τὸ δίκτυον μεστὸν ἦν ἰχθύων μεγάλων ἑκατὸν πεντήκοντα τριῶν.

κυκλόθεν τοῦ θρόνου θρόνοι εἴκοσι τέσσαρες. τὸ ἀρνίον ἑστὸς
ἐπὶ τὸ ὄρος Σιών, καί μετ' αὐτοῦ ἑκατὸν τεσσαράκοντα
τέσσαρες χιλιάδες. συνιόντος δὲ ὄχλου πολλοῦ ἐλαλεῖ πρὸς
αὐτὸν διὰ παραβολῆς.

DEFECTIVE VERBS

237. As in other languages, so in Greek, there are a few verbs
in frequent use which are called 'defective' because they are
found in a limited number of tenses only, the remaining tenses
being drawn from quite different stems; the whole verb—or as
much of it as does actually exist—is thus made up from two or
three different stems. This is so even in English: we have 'I
go' for the pres., but 'I went' for the past historic, as from a
verb no longer used (except in 'to wend one's way'); and so on.

In Greek, the principle still holds good in these defective
verbs—that all pres. tenses, in all the moods, etc., are formed
regularly from the pres. stem, the imperf. always following the
pres. (para. 151 *ad fin.*). It is only the other tenses that have
now to be learnt.

238. ἔρχομαι (I go, come). Imperf., naturally, ἠρχόμην
(temporal augment). The other tenses are from a stem ἐλυθ,
lengthened to ἐλευθ or shortened to ἐλθ. Thus—fut. ind.
ἐλεύσομαι, pres.-perf. ἐλήλυθα, past-perf. ἐλήλυθειν, 2nd aor.
ἦλθον; and so throughout, the appropriate terminations added
to the tense stem.

239. ἐσθίω (I eat). Imperf. ἤσθιον. Other tenses from
φαγ. Thus—fut. ind. φάγομαι, 2nd aor. ἔφαγον.

240. τρέχω (I run). 2nd aor. ind. ἔδραμον, from a stem δρεμ.

241. φέρω (I bear, carry). Fut. ind. οἴσω, from a stem οἰ.

Other tenses are from a stem ἐνεγκ or ἐνεκ. Thus—1st aor. ἤνεγκα, 2nd aor. ἤνεγκον, pres.-perf. ἐνήνοχα (double reduplication); 1st aor. pass. ἠνέχθην.

242. αἱρέω (I take; mid. αἱρέομαι, choose—*i.e.*, take for oneself). This verb is defective only as to the 2nd aor. tenses, which are from a stem ἑλ; ind. act. εἷλον, mid. εἱλόμην; inf. act. ἑλεῖν, mid. ἑλέσθαι. The other tenses are conjugated regularly, allowing for ε being lengthened to η.

243. ὁράω (I see). Imperf. ἑώρων, pres.-perf. ind. ἑώρακα. Two other stems are used in this verb: (1) ὀπ or ὀπτ (cp. ὀφθαλμός)—fut. ind. ὄψομαι, 1st aor. subj. ὄψωμαι, 1st aor. ind. pass. ὤφθην, inf. ὀφθῆναι, fut. pass. ὀφθήσομαι. (2) Ϝιδ (the Ϝ represents the old Greek digamma; cp. the *v* in the Lat. *video* (I see)—2nd aor. εἶδον, ἴδω, ἰδεῖν, ἰδών, 2nd perf. οἶδα, imperat. ἴσθι, subj. εἰδῶ, inf. εἰδέναι, part. εἰδώς, past-perf. ᾔδειν, fut. εἰδήσω.

Once the different stems are recognized, it can be seen that formation is regular, due allowance being made for the temporal augment in the ind. mood, improper reduplication in the perf. tenses, and the needful euphonic changes.

An old imperat. mid., ἴδε, ἰδού, is used as an interjection—'behold!'

The 2nd perf. (with, of course, the primary meaning 'I have seen') came to mean 'I know', and is regularly conjugated as such in the N.T. There were, however, different forms in classical use for the plural, and one of these (ἴσασι) was used by Paul before Agrippa, as reported in Acts 26. 4.

The past-perf., ᾔδειν, then, means 'I knew'.

The above verbs are of the 1st conj. There is one more, completing the list, of the 2nd.

244. φημί (I say). The stem of this verb is φα, and the imperf., therefore, ἔφην. From a stem ἐπ is formed 1st aor. ind. εἶπα, but more frequently 2nd aor. εἶπον. (λέγω is found only in pres. and imperf.). From another stem ἐρ is formed—fut. ἐρέω or ἐρῶ, pres.-perf. εἴρηκα, pass. εἴρημαι; and from yet another, ῥε, is formed 1st aor. pass. ἐρρέθην or ἐρρήθην, part. ῥηθείς.

245. These defective verbs can be compounded with pre-positions in the ordinary way; e.g. from προτρέχω (I run before), 2nd aor. προέδραμον; from ἐξέρχομαι (I depart), fut. ἐξελεύσομαι, 2nd aor. ἐξῆλθον; κατεσθίω (I devour), 2nd aor. κατέφαγον.

ANSWERS TO EXERCISES

1. τὰ δῶρα τοῦ προφήτου. οἱ στρατιῶται τῆς βασιλίσσης. ἡ ζωὴ καὶ ἡ εἰρήνη. αἱ θύραι τοῦ ἱεροῦ. τὰ τέκνα τοῦ προφήτου. ὁ δεσπότης τοῦ οἴκου. αἱ ἐντολαὶ τοῦ Θεοῦ. ὦ βασίλισσα. ὁ σταυρὸς τοῦ Χρίστου. αἱ ἁμαρτίαι τῆς γλώσσης. τὰ δένδρα τῆς γῆς. οἱ λόγοι τῶν διδασκάλων. λέξον τοῖς ἀνθρώποις.

2. ἐν ταῖς νεφέλαις τοῦ οὐρανοῦ. ἡ βασιλεία τῶν οὐρανῶν. ἐν τῇ ὁδῷ τῶν ἐντολῶν τοῦ Θεοῦ. τὸ εὐαγγέλιον τοῦ Ἰησοῦ Χριστοῦ. ὁ μαθητὴς τῷ Ἰησοῦ εἶπεν. ἐν τῷ νόμῳ καὶ τοῖς προφήταις. ἡ ῥάβδος τοῦ προφήτου. αἱ τρίβοι τῆς δικαιοσύνης. ἡ εἰρήνη τοῦ Θεοῦ. ἐν τῇ περιχώρῳ.

3. (A) My sheep are in the wilderness. I am Jehovah your God. I am the way and the truth and the life. Ye are in his Son Jesus Christ. Jesus is the Son of God. I am the Alpha and the Omega. Are we of God? The world is not of God.

(B) τὰ τέκνα αὐτῶν ἐν τῷ οἴκῳ ἐστί. οὐκ ἐν τῇ νήσῳ οἱ υἱοὶ ὑμῶν εἰσι. σὺ εἶ ἐν τῇ βασιλείᾳ τοῦ Θεοῦ. Χριστιανοί ἐσμεν. ἐν ἐξουσίᾳ τὸ εὐαγγέλιον τοῦ Ἰησοῦ Χριστοῦ. τὰ τέκνα τοῦ Θεοῦ ἐν τῇ ὁδῷ τῆς δικαιοσύνης εἰσιν. νεανία, ἡ καρδία σου οὐκ ἔστιν ἐν εἰρήνῃ.

4. (A) Faithful is the word; or, The word is faithful. Eternal life is in the Son of God. The church of God which is in Christ Jesus our Lord. Great is the love of God. The things of God are good. We are not of the evil one.

(B) τὰ μέγαλα τοῦ νόμου μου. ὁ θρόνος τοῦ Θεοῦ ἐν οὐρανῷ [or, τοῖς οὐρανοῖς] ἐστι. ἀγαθὸς ὁ Θεός. οἱ κριταὶ δίκαιοι. τοῖς πιστοῖς ἐν Χριστῷ Ἰησοῦ. ὁ τυφλὸς πρὸ τῆς θύρας τοῦ ἱεροῦ ἐστιν. σὺν τοῖς θηρίοις.

5. (A) The slaves of the wicked one are not good. Great is thy righteousness. Those who are in the kingdom of heaven are not wicked. Our righteousness is not of the law. He is a disciple of the great teacher. Thou art my lord. I have a book. These things said the lord. A great prophet was in that house. After these things.

(B) ἡ δικαιοσύνη σου—ἡ σὴ δ.—ἡ δ. ἡ σή. οἱ υἱοὶ ἡμῶν—οἱ ἡμέτεροι υἱοι—οἱ υἱ. οἱ ἡμέτεροι. τὰ πλοῖα ὑμῶν—τὰ ὑμέτερα πλ.—τὰ πλ. τὰ ὑμέτερα. οἱ μαθηταί μου—οἱ ἐμοὶ μ.—οἱ μ. οἱ ἐμοί.

(C) μεγάλη εἰρήνη ἡμῖν ἦν. ὁ ἄνθρωπος ἐκεῖνος διδάσκαλος μέγας ἔσται. δοῦλος ἦν (ἐγώ*). (ἡμεῖς*) οὐκ ἦμεν ἐν τῇ χώρᾳ ἐκείνῃ. ὁ κύριος ἡμῶν εἶ σύ.

6. (A) οὗτοι υἱοὶ τοῦ Θεοῦ εἰσι. ὁ τοῦ Θεοῦ ἅγιος. τὰ σώματα τῶν ἁγίων. ἡ ἐκκλησία τὸ Χριστοῦ σῶμα ἐστι. Χριστὸς ἡ τῆς ἐκκλησίας κεφαλή ἐστι. ἐν τῷ πνεύματι τοῦ Θεοῦ. τὸ αὐτὸ πνεῦμα. δοῦλος οὔκ εἰμι ἐγὼ τοῦ γράμματος.

(B) Our commonwealth is in *the* heaven*s*. The Holy Spirit of God. Ye yourselves are branches of the heavenly vine. My name is Andrew. The words of his mouth were good. The blood of Jesus Christ God's Son. Large letters are in this book. The spirit itself. Whose is this decree?

7. (A) Great is thy faith. The twelve were with Jesus in a certain city. Thou art with me. A certain man had two sons. Of his kingdom there shall be no end. The body without spirit is dead. On the first day of the year.

(B) πολλὰ τὰ σκεύη τοῦ ἱεροῦ. ἑπτὰ ὄρη ἐν τῇ πόλει τῇ αἰωνίῳ(ᾳ) ἐστίν. μέλη ἐσμεν τοῦ σώματος τοῦ Χριστοῦ. ἡ ἀνάστασις τῶν νεκρῶν. ὦ μέγα ὄρος! τὰ δικαιώματα τοῦ Θεοῦ ἤρχετο (came) διὰ τοῦ στόματος τῶν προφήτων αὐτοῦ. τῷ αὐτῷ ἔτει. ἡ πίστις χωρὶς ἔργων νεκρά ἐστιν.

* If emphasis is intended.

8. (A) I am the good shepherd.   He is a murderer.   After three years.   The ten horns and the seven heads of the beast. Many priests [are] with the king.   There are twelve months in a year.   Therefore none of those scribes shall be with me in my kingdom.   These great wonders shall be in heaven.

(B) οἱ τοῦ τέκνου γονεῖς ἐν τῇ ἁγίᾳ πόλει οὐκ εἰσίν. ὁ Θεὸς ὁ σωτὴρ ἡμῶν ἐστι. οὗτος ἡ δύναμις τοῦ Θεοῦ ἡ μεγάλη ἐστιν. ὁ Θεὸς οὗτος ὁ Θεὸς ἡμῶν εἰς τὸν αἰῶνα ἔσται. ἡ γνῶσις τοῦ Θεοῦ ἡ καλή. τὰ ἔθνη τῆς γῆς πολλά εἰσι. τῷ μήνι τοῦ ἔτους τῷ δωδεκάτῳ. πολλοὶ τυφλοὶ ἐν τῇ ὁδῷ εἰσιν. ποιμὴν εἷς ἔσται.

9. (A) My judgement is just.   This is my father's will.   I am the bread of *the* life.   This saying (*or* word) is hard.   I am the light of the world.   Thou art that man's disciple.   The Father is in me and I [am] in the Father.   In my Father's house are many rooms.   I am the true vine, and my Father is the husbandman.   Of him and through him and unto him [are] all things; to him [is] (*i.e.*, his is) the glory for ever.   These sayings [are] faithful and true.

(B) ἄνδρες, γυναῖκες, καὶ παῖδες (τέκνα) ἐν τῇ πόλει ταύτῃ εἰσί. οὗτοι οἱ λόγοι σκληροί εἰσιν. τὰ πάντα ἐκ τοῦ Θεοῦ ἐστι. εἰρήνη ὑμῖν. οἱ ὄρνιθες τοῦ οὐρανοῦ πολλοί εἰσιν. ὁ πονηρὸς ὁ ἄρχων τοῦ κόσμου τούτου ἐστί. ἐν τῷ θελήματι τοῦ Θεοῦ ἡ εἰρήνη ἡμῶν ἐστιν. ἡ πίστις, ἡ ἐλπίς, καὶ ἡ ἀγάπη.

10. (A) A slave is not greater than his lord (*or* master).   We are witnesses of these things.   I have no children.   I [am] the God of thy fathers.   She is younger than her sister.   The weakness of God is stronger than men.   The sons of this age [are] more prudent than the sons of the light.

(B) ὁ Θεὸς ἰσχυρότερός ἐστιν ἡμῶν (or ἢ ἡμεῖς). οἱ
ἱερεῖς σοφώτεροί εἰσιν. διὰ τοῦτο οἱ υἱοὶ τοῦ Θεοῦ μακαριώ-
τεροι ἢ οἱ τοῦ κόσμου τούτου εἰσίν. φρονιμώτατοί εἰσιν.
εἰρήνη τῷ οἴκῳ τούτῳ.

11. (A) We will remember the words of the Lord Jesus. He
has killed a man. A certain man has shaken the doors of the
temple. His seven daughters were prophesying (or used to
prophesy). All the good priests fasted in the days of the law.
We believe in God the Saviour of all men. All men did not
believe in *the* Jesus. We will serve thee, O king. He had
planted a vineyard. They will prophesy in those days.

(B) βασιλεύσουσιν ἐπὶ τῆς γῆς. σαλεύσω τοὺς οὐρανοὺς καὶ
τὴν γῆν. θεράπευσει τὸν υἱόν μου. πιστεύεις τῷ Θεῷ;
θύουσιν τῷ Θεῷ τῷ ἀληθινῷ. οὐ νηστεύομεν ἐν ταυταῖς ταῖς
ἡμεραῖς.

12. (A) I and the Father are one [note the neuter form of the
numeral here—one thing, *not* one person]. This man had
four daughters, and they used to prophesy. I will heal him.
The Jesus healed the man. God anointed *the* Jesus of [*lit.*
from] Nazareth with *the* Holy Spirit and power. Glory [be]
to the Father, and to the Son, and to the Holy Spirit. The
girl is not blind. The lion's ears [are] large, but the boy's
teeth are small. The disciples remembered the words of Jesus.
The mother of *the* Jesus was there. This husbandman has
planted a tree in his garden.

(B) οὐ νηστεύσομεν ἐν τῷ καιρῷ ἐκείνῳ. οἱ πόδες τοῦ
προβάτου οὐκ εἰσι μεγάλοι. αὐτὴν τεθεράπευκα. πιστεύω
τῷ Θεῷ. πιστεύομεν εἰς τὸν Θεὸν πατέρα. ὑμεῖς πιστεύετε
τὸν κύριον Ἰησοῦν; τῷ Θεῷ δουλεύομεν ἐν τῷ πνεύματι
ἡμῶν. ἐνήστευον ἐν τῷ ἱερῷ. ἐφονεύσαμεν αὐτόν. οὐκ
ἐπίστευσαν αὐτοῦ τοῖς λόγοις. δουλεύετε τὸν κύριον χριστόν.

13. (A) Loose ye him. A man planted a vineyard. Remember ye my words. Believe ye in *the* God, and believe in me. Lament thou not, only believe. The Pharisees used to fast. He shall reign over the house of Jacob for ever, and of his kingdom there shall be no end. Dismiss her, master. Jesus wept.

(B) τοὺς ὄχλους ἀπόλυσον, κύριε. προφήτευσον, βασιλεῦ τῶν Ἰουδαίων. οἱ τοῦ Ζεβεδαίου υἱοὶ ἐνήστευσαν τῇ ἡμέρᾳ ἐκείνῃ. οὐ πιστεύετέ μοι; νηστευέτωσαν. μὴ κλαιέτω. οὐκ ἐμνημονεύσατε τῶν λόγων μου; θεράπευσόν με, ὦ κύριε. κέχρικε τὸν υἱόν μου. κλεῖσον τὴν θύραν.

14. (A) Let us not lament. Believe ye not his words. Did I believe him? O woman, great is thy faith. I have much people in this city. Jesus healed many men. Thou shalt by no means reign over my people. Certain women believed Jesus. We believe in order that we may serve the Lord. Anoint thou him that he may prophesy. Let us not kill them.

(B) πιστεύσατε τῷ εὐαγγελίῳ, ἵνα ἔχητε αἰώνιον ζωήν. μὴ μνημονεύωμεν τῶν κακῶν ῥημάτων αὐτοῦ. μὴ πιστεύομεν τῷ λόγῳ; οὐ μὴ θεραπεύσῃς τὸν ἄνδρα. γυναῖκες πολλαὶ ἐν τῇ πόλει ἔκλαιον. οἱ ἄνθρωποι οὐκ ἔκλεισαν τὴν θύραν. μὴ δουλεύωμεν τῷ πονηρῷ. φυτευσάτω τὰ δένδρα. πολλά μοί ἐστιν. οὐ νηστεύσετε. μὴ νηστευέτωσαν. προφήτευσον, ἄνθρωπε.

15. (A) I know whom I have believed [with a continuing faith]. We ourselves have heard his voice. This is the message which we have heard from him. Beloved, believe not this spirit. Many false prophets are in the world. We are witnesses of these things. Ye shall be my witnesses both in Jerusalem and in *the* Judæa.

(B) οἱ λόγοι τῶν μαρτύρων ὧν ἠκούσαμεν δίκαιοι ἦσαν. ὁ μαθητὴς οὗ ἤκουσαν τυφλός ἐστι. ὑμεῖς ἠκούσατε αὐτοὶ τὴν

φωνὴν αὐτοῦ ἐν τῇ πολεῖ τῇ ἁγίᾳ. ἀκουσάτωσαν ὃ αὐτοῖς
λέγει.

16. (A) As he sowed. While men slept. God has commanded men to believe his holy gospel. I tell you not to weep.
It is good to serve Jehovah. Jesus commanded the twelve to
remember his words.

(B) οὐκ ἔστι καλὸν λατρεύειν τῷ πονηρῷ. ὁ χριστὸς οὐκ
ἐκέλευσε νηστεύειν τοὺς μαθητὰς αὐτοῦ.

(C) Christ did not command us to fast. Christ commanded
us not to fast.

17. The strong [ἰσχύω = I am strong] have no need of a
physician, but those who are ill. Why do we and the Pharisees
fast, but thy disciples fast not? He who hears my word has
eternal life. Those who believe not the words of *the* Jesus
have not the life of the ages. He who has an ear, let him hear
what the Spirit says to the churches.

18. Lovest thou me? Ye are the salt of the earth and the
light of the world. He who hates me hates my Father also.
Blessed are those who hunger and thirst [after] *the* righteousness. The world has hated me. Because I have said these
things to you, *the* sorrow has filled your heart. They have
kept thy word. Let us love one another. Holy Father, keep
them in thy name. Thou art Peter, and on this rock I will
build my church, and hell's gates shall not prevail against it.
Good teacher, what shall I do to inherit (*lit.* what doing, *or*
having done, may I inherit) eternal life? Thou shalt love
Jehovah thy God.

19. (A) All who believe in the name of *the* Jesus Christ are
in his kingdom. My church shall be built [οἰκοδομέω] on this
rock. All things are mine. This man built our synagogue.

The children [are] unwilling. Everyone who hears my voice hears also the Father. The sons of God are led by his Spirit. His commandments are not grievous [*lit.* heavy]. I was led, *or* being led, by the Spirit of Jesus. Our gospel was believed.

(B) ἠγόμεθα, φιληθήσεσθε, πιστεύεται, ἄγῃ.

20. Be thou silenced (φιμόω). Be silenced [and remain so; the perf. imperat. is comparatively rare in N.T., but such is its force]. Ye greatly err (πλανάω, in pass. 'I err') [the neut. πολύ is used adverbially—see para. 103]. Thou art the Son of the living God. Saints shall reign with (συμβασιλεύω) Christ. He is not a God of dead persons, but of living [ones]. We deceive ourselves. After these things a rich man from Arimathæa, Joseph by name [*lit.* the (= his) name J.], who also himself followed (μαθητεύω) *the* Jesus, asked for (αἰτέω) the body of Jesus. *The* Paul passed through (διοδεύω = διά + ὁδεύω) *the* Amphipolis. The wind and the sea obeyed him. An angel from heaven strengthened (ἐνισχύω) *the* Jesus.

21. He shall be called a Nazarene. They shall be called sons of God. Be not ye called rabbi, neither be ye called leaders. Thou, child, shalt be called a prophet of *the* Most High. Go to thy house; thy son lives. I will go to my father. Thou who teachest another, teachest thou not thyself? They feared the people. Not one of those men shall taste of my supper. Fear ye not them. *The* Jesus was teaching in one of their synagogues. The blood of Jesus Christ, God's Son, cleanses us from all sin. He who hears my words and believes in me shall by no means taste of death.

22. Look on, *or* at, us. What thou seest write in a book and send to the seven churches. Moses wrote concerning Jesus. What I have written, I have written. Now concerning the things of which ye wrote to me. So persecuted they the

prophets who were before you. Why persecutest thou me? Ye shall be persecuted from city to city. He shall teach you all things. The God of *the* peace shall bruise Satan under your feet shortly. We fed thee. Pharaoh's daughter brought up Moses as her own son [*lit.* to herself for a son]. Turn to him also the other cheek. I beseech thee, therefore, father, that thou wouldest send Lazarus to my father's house; for I have five brothers.

23. The Spirit of *the* truth shall glorify me. He glorified the God of Israel. Glorify thy name. I am glorified in them. Lord, save us. Thou shalt call his name Jesus, for he shall save his people from their sins. Thy faith has saved thee. The woman was healed. I am saying these things, in order that ye may be saved. Others he saved, let him save himself. I bought five yoke of oxen. These he named apostles. The unbelieving husband is sanctified by the wife, and the unbelieving wife is sanctified by the brother.

24. Are we stronger than the Lord [that is, We are not . . ., are we]? The foolishness of God is wiser than men, and the weakness of God is stronger than men. The exceeding great and precious promises. The first treatise I made, most excellent Theophilus. There shall be joy in heaven over one sinner repenting [more] than over ninety-nine just men who have no need of repentance. He who prophesies is greater than he who speaks in tongues. Now is our salvation nearer than when we believed. We have the prophetic word more secure. For both he who sanctifies and those who are sanctified [are] all of one. His elder son was in [the] field. I am no longer worthy to be called thy son; make me as one of thy hired servants. Greater is he who is in you than he that is in the world. Everyone who believes that Jesus is the Christ is begotten of God, and everyone who loves him who begat loves him who is begotten of him.

25. Let them flee to the mountains. They shall by no means escape. They all fled. If any one of you lacks wisdom, let him ask from God. I prayed concerning thee, that thy faith should not fail. Let us go hence. He will gather his wheat into the garner, but the chaff he will consume with unquenchable fire. Gather ye together the fragments which remain. Thou shalt have treasure in heaven. There were many lamps in the upper room where we were gathered. They had a few fishes. Her little daughter had an unclean spirit.

26. Now after these things Joseph of (*lit.* from) Arimathæa, being a disciple of Jesus, but hidden because of fear of the Jews, requested Pilate. I hid thy talent in the earth. Your life is hid with *the* Christ in *the* God. The Word became flesh and tabernacled among us. The magi, falling down, worshipped the child Jesus. The house fell, and its fall was great. Fall ye on us. Let him take heed (*lit.* see) lest he fall. *The* love never fails. Let thy will come to pass. The first angel sounded a trumpet. I saw a star fallen out of heaven to the earth. Let it happen to thee as thou believedst. *The* God becomes a rewarder to those who seek him out.

27. We have never yet served anyone [note the different position of the negative]. For all sinned and come short [= coming short] of the glory of God. By *the* love serve ye one another. Learn ye from me. This only I desire to learn from you—did ye receive the Spirit by works of law or by hearing of faith? But as many as received him became God's children. The Spirit of *the* truth shall glorify me, because he shall receive of that which is mine. The kingdom of *the* heaven*s* is like leaven, which a woman took and hid in three measures of meal till the whole was leavened. Handle not, neither taste, nor touch.

28. The lord commanded him to be sold, and his (*lit.* the) wife, and his children, and all things whatever he had (*lit.* has—see para. 205). But I am carnal, sold under *the* sin. God, be propitiated to me. Let each of you please his (*lit.* the) neighbour with a view to that which is good unto edification. I do not seek to please men. No one fully knows the Son except the Father. The world came into being through him, and the world knew him not. Knowest thou what things thou readest? For there is nothing hidden which shall not become manifest, nor covered which shall not be known. Remember ye my bonds. Let him who reads understand. This title therefore many of the Jews read.

29. But this man did nothing amiss. Let not your heart be troubled, neither let it be afraid. Lord, open to us. Thou doest the same things. For Adam was formed first, then Eve. What are ye about to do? Jesus, remember me. Christ suffered on our behalf. Knock, and it shall be opened to you. He who hates his life in this world shall keep it unto life eternal. Even though he was a son, he learned *the* obedience from the things which he suffered. Teacher, all these things I kept from my youth. I heard a strong angel proclaiming with a loud voice.

30. They washed their robes and whitened them in the blood of the Lamb. They were washing their nets. Cast thyself down. Now the day began to decline. *The* perfect love casts out *the* fear. Judge not, lest ye be judged. Mary the Magdalene comes announcing to the disciples that she had seen the Lord. Abide with us, because it is toward evening, and the day has now declined.

31. Thus it was necessary for the Christ to suffer. The labouring husbandman must first receive of the fruits. What

must I do in order that I may be saved? The hireling cares not for the sheep. Gallio cared for none of these things. It is lawful to do well on the sabbath days. For John said [note imperf. = said repeatedly] to Herod, It is not lawful for thee to have thy brother's wife. What think ye concerning the Christ? What thinkest thou, Simon? Is it fitting for a woman to pray to God uncovered? For such a high priest was fitting for us, holy, harmless, undefiled. Those sent were of the Pharisees. Again he sent other slaves.

32. Slaves, obey ye with fear and trembling the (= your) masters according to [the] flesh. They did not all obey the gospel. They worshipped and served the creature rather than the Creator, who is blessed for ever. Fill the waterpots with water. Peter, turning, sees the disciple whom Jesus loved following, who also leaned on his breast at the supper. Remember Jesus Christ.

33. I beseech thee, lady, not as writing a new commandment to thee, but [one] which we had from the beginning, that we love one another. Think on these things, be thou in them, that thy progress may be manifest to all. They besought him that they might only touch the fringe of his garment. Jesus expelled the spirits with a word, and all who were ill he healed; so that that which was spoken through the prophet was fulfilled. Pray ye therefore the lord of the harvest that he thrust forth workmen into his harvest. Then the Pharisees went and took counsel so that they might ensnare him in word. To which end also we pray always concerning you, that our God may count you worthy of the calling, and may fulfil every good pleasure of goodness, so that the name of our Lord Jesus may be glorified in you.

34. I lay down my life on behalf of the sheep. Leading up *the* Jesus, the devil showed him all the kingdoms of the world

in a moment of time.   I will give thee all this authority and
their glory, for it has been delivered to me, and to whomever I
will I give it. Show thyself to the priest. He will show you an
upper room.   Show me a denarius.   I will show thee the
things which must happen after these things.   Ask, and it shall
be given to you.   The moon shall not give her light.   The law
was given through Moses, *the* grace and *the* truth came through
Jesus Christ.   So, my beloved, with fear and trembling, work
out your own salvation.

35. Give to him who asks thee.   Give us today our daily
bread.   Give not that which is holy to the dogs.   It is given
to you to know the mysteries of the kingdom of God.   The
multitudes were awestruck and glorified *the* God who gave
such authority to *the* men.   Is it lawful to give tribute to
Cæsar or no?   Calling his twelve disciples, he gave them
authority of (= over) unclean spirits, to expel them, and to heal
every disease and every sickness.   Give us day by day [note
tense as compared with earlier sentence] our daily bread.   Let
us give the glory to him.

36. The devil says to Jesus, If thou art God's Son, throw
thyself down.   If I do this willingly, I have a reward; but if
unwillingly, I am entrusted with a stewardship.   If then ye
were raised with *the* Christ, seek the things [which are] above.
If they cannot restrain themselves, let them marry.   There they
placed the body of Jesus.   Those who heard these words put
[= laid them up] in their heart.   Where have ye laid him?
God was in Christ reconciling the world to himself, not
reckoning to them their trespasses, and placing in us the word
of *the* reconciliation.   Why didst thou determine [the middle
voice of τίθημι has this meaning] this thing in thy heart?   I
have constituted thee a father of many nations.   Kneeling
down, *the* Jesus prayed, saying, Father, if thou willest, take

away this cup from me; nevertheless not my will but thine be done.

37. If anyone keep my word, he shall never taste death. If anyone thirst, let him come to me and drink. If the uncircumcision keep the ordinances of the law, shall not its uncircumcision be reckoned as circumcision? She shall be saved through childbearing, if they continue in faith and love and sanctification with sobriety. If the house be worthy, let your peace come upon it. Calling a child to him, Jesus set him in their midst. He shall set the sheep on his right hand, but the goats on the left. How shall his kingdom stand?

38. But even if we or an angel out of heaven should preach a gospel to you besides that which we preached to you, let him be a curse. Again I say, if anyone preaches you a gospel besides that which ye received, let him be a curse. Resist not evil (*or* the evil man). Quench not the Spirit. Render the things of Cæsar to Cæsar, and the things of God to God. Our lamps are being extinguished. He will render to each one according to his works. Behold, I stand at the door and knock. Knowing the grace given to me, James and Cephas and John gave to me and Barnabas the right hands of fellowship. Thou [emphatic] standest by *the* faith. He will not quench smouldering flax. Gird thyself.

39. The axe lies at the root of the trees. A city lying on a mountain cannot be hidden. Ye know not the things of the morrow. Lord, they know that I was guarding and beating throughout the synagogues those who believe on thee. Cursed is everyone who hangs on a tree. A sound filled all the house where they were sitting. We cannot deny [it]. If thou canst do anything, help us and have compassion on us. An angel of Jehovah descending from heaven rolled away the stone and sat on it.

40. Then the devil leaves him. If ye forgive men their trespasses, your heavenly Father will also forgive you. Leave there thy gift before the altar. The fever left her. The Son of man has authority on *the* earth to forgive sins. Leave both to grow together until the harvest. Your house is being left to you desolate. He did not allow the demons to speak. Thou hast left thy first love.

41. In [the] fifteenth year of the governorship of Tiberius Cæsar. Forty-six years this temple was built (*i.e.* the building then began). The net was full of great fishes, a hundred and fifty-three. Around the throne were twenty-four thrones. The Lamb stood on *the* Mount Sion, and with him a hundred and forty-four thousand. And a great crowd accompanying [him], he spoke to them by means of a parable.

gender § 20, 32,
common gender § 32

INDEX